GREAT WESTERN STYLE

Kevin McCormack

Rails

Acknowledgements

The images in this book come from a variety of sources but are mostly from the collections held by Online Transport Archive, a charity created to preserve transport photographs, negatives and cine film. Wherever possible, the photographer has been acknowledged but in a few cases it has not been possible to identify the source such as monochrome unmarked prints acquired some fifty years ago. Several pictures used were taken by me and I am also grateful to various individuals for allowing me access to their own material or photograph collections: Bob Bridger (for use of Charles Firminger's photographs), Björn Larsson, Dave Robinson, Tony Hisgett, Alan Sainty, Bruce Jenkins, Nigel Hunt and Martin Jenkins. Special thanks goes to Frank Dumbleton (Great Western Society Marketing Department) and Laurence Waters of the Didcot-based Great Western Trust for their valuable assistance. The abbreviation LRTA refers to the Light Rail Transit Association, London Branch. Finally, I must thank my daughter Miranda Fair for her computer skills in organising the material for publication.

Above The GWR's most powerful express locomotive class is represented by King class 4-6-0 No 6027 *King Richard I* at Leamington Spa on 3 March 1931. *Transport Treasury*

Title page: Great Western Style is epitomised in this view of a "push and pull" (auto train) service even though the steel-bodied trailer (W241W) was built by BR, albeit to a GWR outline. The locomotive is Collett 0-4-2 tank No 1466, now preserved by the GWS at Didcot. The photograph was taken on 21 February 1959 between Pullabrook and Lustleigh in Devon and depicts the 12.50pm train from Newton Abbot to Moretonhampstead, exactly one week before withdrawal of passenger services on the branch. *Les Folkard/ Online Transport Archive*

Rear cover Some seven years into Nationalisation, the tender of Hall class 4-6-0 No 6990 *Witherslack Hall* still proudly displays its GWR origins in this view at Old Oak Common on 28 November 1954. Ironically, this locomotive was completed in April 1948 and therefore had British Railways emblazoned on its original tender. However, as a brand new engine No 6990 was selected as a mixed traffic representative for the Locomotive Exchanges of 1948 working on the Eastern Region, and the former GWR hierarchy decided that it should run with a tender carrying GWR livery, so the tender was swopped with one from another engine. By coincidence this locomotive is now in service on the heritage Great Central Railway, operating over part of the line on which it ran in 1948. *Author's collection*

First published 2018

Published by Rails Publishing
www.capitaltransport.com

Printed by Parksons Graphics

Loosely based on the GWR's 1930s Speed to the West poster, British Railways (Western Region) still featured an image of a King class locomotive designed in 1926-7 instead of a new diesel hydraulic on this 1960 timetable! *Author's collection*

Contents

Introduction

This book in the Style series covers the much loved Great Western Railway ("GWR"), depicting its uniqueness, traditions and style through a collection of images, mostly previously unpublished and, from the 1950s onwards, depicted in colour during the time when the GWR's image was perpetuated by the nationalised entity, British Railways (Western Region) (BR(W). It is testament to the widespread respect held for the GWR, a company which officially ceased to exist on 1 January 1948, that the current Train Operating Company providing passenger services over much of the former GWR network rebranded itself from First Great Western to Great Western Railway in 2015. So the GWR lives again!

The GWR can be credited with a number of "firsts" in Britain, some examples being:

- Train travel by a Reigning Monarch
- Special postal trains
- Use of corridor carriages
- Introduction of 4-6-2 and 2-8-0 locomotives
- Inauguration of motor bus services by a standard-gauge railway company
- Reaching 100mph (but claim disputed, as is Flying Scotsman's later claim!)
- Operation of scheduled air services by a railway company
- First streamlined locomotives (albeit a half-hearted attempt!)
- First locomotive testing plant in Europe

Various unique features are also associated with the GWR, some examples of which are:

- Use of Broad Gauge on main lines
- World's first regular use of surface train warning system (ATC)
- World's longest regular non-stop railway service at the time
- World's fastest train journey at the time
- Sole major railway company to retain its identity at the Grouping in 1923
- Only railway company to avoid the renumbering of its locomotives by BR
- GWR style livery adopted by BR for steam passenger locomotives
- Britain's longest mainline railway tunnel (Severn)
- Last BR steam locomotive built at ex-GWR Swindon Works
- BR corporate blue livery applied to only three steam locomotives, all ex-GWR
- Ex-GWR locomotive inaugurated the "Return to Steam" in 1971
- Ex-GWR locomotive chosen for the Harry Potter films and now world famous
- Most prolific user of "slip" coaches (detaching them at speed from express trains for intermediate stations)

By way of brief background, the origins of the GWR lay in Bristol where, in 1832, a group of merchants met to consider the building of a railway line to London and to obtain funding for a survey to be carried out. After advertising for an engineer, they appointed, in 1833, 27-year old Isambard Kingdom Brunel who, despite his relative youth, was known in Bristol, especially through his designs for the Clifton Suspension Bridge. The railway company was originally to be called "The Bristol and London Railway" but it seems to have been Brunel who decided on the name "Great Western Railway" in the belief that "his" railway would be superior to other railways and would eventually extend beyond London-Bristol. Brunel

Railway enthusiasts will probably consider the most famous GWR engine to be *City of Truro* or *King George V* but, in the wider world, their fame is surpassed by Barry scrapyard escapee No 5972 *Olton Hall*, in its guise as *Hogwarts Castle* – the Hall class locomotive that has become a Castle! Owned by West Coast Railways, No 5972, in its Harry Potter role, can be viewed at Warner Bros Studios, Leavesden, Hertfordshire. *elisfkc Wikimedia Commons, Hogwarts Express (16658835527)*

regarded speed of travel as a very important factor in his design work, hence his adoption of a broad gauge of 7ft 0¼ins and the construction of cuttings, embankments, tunnels, bridges etc to ensure that the line was as level as possible, with no sharp curves. Parliamentary approval for the railway was granted in 1835 and the first section (from just outside Paddington to the outskirts of Maidenhead) was opened in 1838, with the entire route to Bristol being completed in 1841.

Brunel's engineering expertise did not, however, extend to locomotives, as evidenced by his early efforts on this front, so Brunel recruited 20-year old Daniel Gooch in 1837 to the position of Superintendent of Locomotive Engines. Gooch immediately purchased two locomotives from Robert Stephenson & Company, one of which (*North Star*) hauled the inaugural train. Gooch went on to design several successful locomotive classes until stepping down in 1864 and becoming GWR Chairman in the following year, a post he held until his death in 1889. He was created a baronet in 1866, becoming Sir Daniel Gooch.

It is worth mentioning here that on 13 June 1842 Queen Victoria became the first British reigning monarch to travel by rail, boarding a broad gauge GWR train at Slough (the two branches to Windsor had not yet been built) and travelling to the first Paddington station at Bishops Road Bridge. The journey time was an astounding 25 minutes, a credit both to the broad gauge and to the fact that the Firefly-class locomotive was being driven by Brunel, with Gooch also on the footplate. On 13 June 2017, to mark the 175th anniversary, HM The Queen recreated the journey by GWR (the new entity) accompanied by descendents of Brunel and Gooch (but neither was driving!). On this occasion the journey, by prototype bi-modal (electric/diesel) unit, took 19 minutes, demonstrating that 175 years of progress had achieved a 6 minute saving!

To return to Locomotive Superintendents, the position subsequently being called Locomotive, Carriage and Wagon Superintendent and eventually Chief Mechanical Engineer (CME), Daniel Gooch was succeeded in 1864 by Joseph Armstrong, who had to cope with the rapid expansion of the GWR network and the gradual reduction of the broad gauge in favour of the standard gauge. Armstrong died suddenly in harness in 1877 and was replaced by his chief assistant, William Dean, whose tenure lasted until 1902. Dean's chief assistant, George Jackson Churchward, then took over and developed outstanding innovative locomotive designs, exemplified by the Saint and Star classes, which formed the basis of the types that lasted until the end of Western Region steam in 1965. Churchward was succeeded by Charles Collett in 1922 who enhanced Churchward's designs by creating such iconic classes as the Kings, Castles and Halls. The GWR's final CME was Frederick Hawksworth who "reigned" from 1941 until the GWR's demise on 31 December 1947 and who is best remembered for his Modified Hall and County 4-6-0 locomotives, as well as his very powerful Pannier tanks.

The progress of the GWR through these successive Locomotive Superintendents/CMEs, and the various styles adopted by the Company, are captured in the pictures, with detailed captions, which follow this Introduction. It should be mentioned, however, that some of the "styles" depicted were in fact inherited by the GWR after it had taken over various minor lines from previously independent companies.

GWR enthusiasts are very fortunate to be able to see Great Western Style through the large number of heritage railways operating on former GWR lines, as well as railway centres and museums featuring GWR stock, buildings, artefacts, etc. The fact that there are so many preserved GWR locomotives is largely due to the fact that Dai Woodham hoarded them in his scrapyard at Barry in South Wales, concentrating on the scrapping of wagons instead of immediately breaking up the engines, and was able to sell them on to preservationists.

My own interest in the GWR stems from the fact that I lived close to the BR(W) mainline at Ealing, West London, for most of the first twenty-five years of my life and became an early member of what later became the Great Western Society (GWS). During the late 1960s/early 1970s I served on the GWS Management Council and in 1972 purchased a very original body of a Dean 6-wheeled Third Class saloon coach (No 2511/9317) which was part of a Thames-side bungalow. I had it mounted on the correct type of GWR underframe in the following year. The photograph opposite taken by Tony Hisgett on 4 May 2010 during Didcot's celebration of the GWR's 175th Anniversary shows the carriage attached to Bill Parker's small prairie tank No 5521 (aka London Transport L150) which took Great Western Style to Europe in 2007-8 when it hauled commuter trains in Poland and piloted the Orient Express.

Broad Gauge

Although aware that other pioneer railway companies were using a track gauge of 4ft 8½ins (adopted by George Stephenson based on the width of wagon wheels), Brunel was convinced that a much wider gauge would enable increasingly powerful locomotives to travel at considerably greater speeds and therefore adopted a 7ft 0¼in gauge which came to be known as the Broad Gauge. George Stephenson is said to have pointed out to Brunel that he should adopt the narrower gauge (subsequently called the Standard Gauge) because eventually all the railways would be joined up. However, Brunel would not be swayed despite the extra costs involved, believing that the Broad Gauge would limit the likelihood of other railway companies infiltrating the GWR's territory. In the short term, Brunel's plans were very successful, the GWR gaining an unrivalled reputation for speed in the 1840s and 1850s. For a few years from 1845, a Paddington-Exeter service, later named the *Flying Dutchman*, was the fastest train in the world, making the journey in 4½ hrs. Among other speed achievements was a non-stop run in 1846 over the 53-mile distance between Paddington to Didcot taking some 50 minutes and in 1848 a timing of 47½ minutes was obtained, with an average speed of 67 mph, the fastest rail journey ever made at that time.

The Government of the day was not however unduly impressed with the broad gauge speed argument, being more concerned with the burden and inconvenience of the transfer of passengers and goods between trains of different gauges. Given that, by the mid-1840s there were more standard gauge lines than broad gauge ones, an Act was passed in 1846 requiring all new railway lines in Great Britain (not Ireland) to be standard gauge and confining the broad gauge to south west England and Wales. Whereas the GWR had been cross-working with, or actually acquiring, other railway companies which also used the broad gauge, it was now starting to acquire railways which were standard gauge, eg in the Midlands, and to minimise train changing began to install a "third rail" inside the broad gauge tracks to allow standard gauge trains to travel over broad gauge lines, this "mixed gauge" reaching Paddington in 1861. Before long the GWR had to face the inevitable fact that the broad gauge was doomed and began the changeover to standard gauge, starting as early as 1866. Final abandonment occurred in May 1892 when the west of England mainline from Paddington was converted.

This is Didcot Railway Centre on 19 April 2014 with two replica broad gauge locomotives based there standing on original bridge rail discovered by the GWS at Burlescome in Devon. On the left is the GWS's *Fire Fly*, representing the first locomotive designed by Daniel Gooch in 1840, when it is claimed to have travelled the 30¾ miles from Twyford to Paddington in 37 minutes. A 2-2-2 with a single centre driving wheel of 7ft diameter, it was the first of a class of 62 engines, one of which hauled the inaugural Royal Train in 1842. On the right is the National Railway Museum's *Iron Duke*, representing a class of Gooch 4-2-2 singles with an 8ft driving wheel, capable of reaching 80mph. The original *Iron Duke* entered service in 1847. In the background is the 1850s broad/narrow gauge Transfer Shed re-erected by the GWS following removal from its original location beside the mainline just west of Didcot station. *Frank Dumbleton*

Left Based on the Gooch Iron Duke class Joseph Armstrong designed the Rover class of 4-2-2 locomotives, this example being *Dragon* pictured at Maidenhead. Taking its name from an Iron Duke locomotive withdrawn in 1872, *Dragon* was built in 1880 and hauled the last broad gauge train from London to Penzance on 20 May 1892. *Great Western Trust*

Below The inconvenience of the "break of gauge" for passengers is highlighted at Didcot's Transfer Shed in this re-enactment featuring *Iron Duke*. The scene is based on a contemporary print depicting chaos at Gloucester station when the broad gauge Bristol-Gloucester railway met the standard gauge Birmingham-Gloucester railway in 1844. This actual Transfer Shed was used for the movement of freight between the gauges, with the two portals being of different sizes, one wider than the other. *Frank Dumbleton*

Above Firefly and replica coaches are seen here in action on mixed gauge track at Didcot. The open carriage was for third class passengers whereas second class passengers were at least provided with a roofed vehicle. *Frank Dumbleton*

Right "The largest pair of wheels on the GWR" (according to the notice) stand at Swindon Works in the late 1950s. They belong to 4-2-2 Single *Lord of the Isles*, the last member of the Iron Duke class to remain in service, which operated from 1851 to 1887. The engine was then preserved by the GWR and exhibited at various events including the Chicago World Fair of 1893. Unfortunately it was scrapped in 1906 along with the original *North Star* from 1837. A replica of the latter, containing a few original parts but without a tender, was constructed by the GWR for the Stockton & Darlington Railway Centenary in 1925 and this locomotive, together with the wheels of *Lord of the Isles*, is now preserved in Steam Museum, Swindon. *Harry Luff/Online Transport Archive*

Above A Rover class 4-2-2 passes Bathampton Junction heading east on an up working of the *Flying Dutchman*. The mainline has been converted to mixed gauge but the branch to Bradford-on-Avon and Westbury on the left is still broad gauge. *Great Western Trust*

Left Another Rover class 4-2-2 speeds along on mixed gauge track. The most obvious outward difference between this class and the earlier Iron Duke locomotives is the protection provided to the footplate crew. In the latter days of the broad gauge, locomotives and rolling stock were built as "convertibles", ie to standard gauge but running on broad gauge frames and wheels prior to conversion. This is illustrated by the first vehicle behind the engine. *Great Western Trust*

Brunel's Legacy

Brunel is generally regarded as the finest engineer of the Victorian era. Indeed, when over a million people voted in a poll in 2002 to find the Greatest Briton of all time, Brunel came second only to Sir Winston Churchill.

Isambard Kingdom Brunel was born in 1806 in Britain Street, Portsea (Portsmouth), taking his first name from the middle name of his French father (Marc Isambard Brunel) and his middle name from the maiden name of his English mother (Sophia Kingdom). He started his working life employed by his father and was appointed resident engineer to drive a tunnel under the River Thames between Rotherhithe and Wapping. After a flood in the tunnel in 1828 which nearly killed him, Brunel left this project and went on to submit various designs for the Clifton Suspension Bridge in Bristol, one of which was accepted in 1831 (although construction was delayed until 1864). He was also an adviser to the Bristol Dock Company so was well known in that area for his engineering experience when he was appointed Engineer of the GWR in 1833 (two years before the GWR Bill received Royal Assent).

Among his many engineering achievements the GWR is probably his most enduring, the gentle curves and gradients of his original London-Bristol line being well suited to today's high speed trains. Many of the structures designed by him are still fulfilling their original role today. Notable examples, proceeding westwards, include Paddington Station, Wharncliffe viaduct (Hanwell), "Three Bridges" (Brentford branch, Southall), Thames Bridge (Windsor), Thames Bridge (Maidenhead), Sonning Cutting, Mortimer Station (Reading-Basingstoke line), Thames Bridge (Basildon/ Gatehampton), Thames Bridge (Moulsford), Silly Bridge (Cholsey), Culham Station (Didcot-Oxford line), Chippenham Viaduct, Box Tunnel, Bristol Temple Meads (original part) and the Royal Albert Bridge (Plymouth/ Saltash). Photographs of some of these examples follow.

This view from April 1964 depicts Hawksworth pannier tank No 9406 standing under Brunel's elegant arches in Paddington station having brought in empty stock from Old Oak Common carriage sidings. *Roy Hobbs/Online Transport Archive*

The first Paddington station opened in 1838 at Bishops Road Bridge, to the west of the present terminus which was designed by Brunel with the assistance of his architect friend, Digby Wyatt, and completed in 1854. The first station had quickly proved inadequate for the increasing volume of railway traffic but quite soon the new station was also found to require more space for the expansion of services. Initially, more platforms were provided by removing the various empty stock sidings within the station, and relocating these elsewhere. However, when there was no further space for expansion, an additional roof span was built to conform as closely as possible to Brunel's original three spans, the new platforms within the fourth span being put into use between 1913 and 1915. The new span is visible on the left of the smokebox of recently-built Castle class 4-6-0 No 5037 *Monmouth Castle* seen in about 1936. This locomotive hauled the last GWR train out of Paddington, the 1150pm to Plymouth, on 31 December 1947. Ten minutes later the original GWR ceased to exist. *Author's collection*

Above Brunel's four railway bridges across the River Thames are still in use but this one at Windsor, on the GWR branch line from Slough, is untypical in not being built in brick. In fact it is his oldest surviving wrought-iron bridge, dating from 1849, although some modifications were made in 1908. *WyrdLight.com/Wiki Commons*

Below Brunel's best known Thames bridge is this one at Maidenhead, made famous because, at the time of construction (1838), the two main arches were the widest and flattest in the world and Brunel's critics were convinced that the bridge would collapse. To allow for track quadrupling, the bridge was widened on both sides after the additional rails had reached the eastern side of the bridge in 1884. Brunel's bridge is Grade II Listed but the one visible in the distance (the road bridge) is Grade I Listed and was built in 1777. *Nancy/Wiki Commons*

Above This four-arch Brunel structure, Basildon (Gatehampton) Bridge between Pangbourne and Goring & Streatley, was built in 1839 and widened on the downstream (eastern) side in 1890 to enable quadrupling of the track. *Nancy/Wiki Commons*

Below Each of Brunel's three brick Thames bridges was widened for track quadrupling in different ways: Maidenhead by widening on both sides, Basildon by widening on one side only and Moulsford (seen here) by the building in 1892 of a closely matching separate bridge 9ft apart from the original 1839 structure. The original bridge is distinguishable by the wedges of Bath stone outlining the four arches whereas the arches of the new bridge are outlined by rings of brickwork. All three bridges now carry overhead electrification structures. *Rod Allday/Wiki Commons/geograph.org.uk-950246*

Left Box Tunnel in Wiltshire, between Chippenham and Bath, is some 1¾ miles long and, when completed in 1841, was the longest tunnel in the world. As ever, Brunel ignored his detractors who argued that the tunnel would be dangerous and impractical (although it was dangerous for the construction workers, some one hundred losing their lives due to the use of explosives for blasting and flooding). This view, probably dating from the inter-war period, shows the classically-designed western portal. *Great Western Trust*

Above This is Culham station between Didcot and Oxford in early 1970 and is an example of a Brunel-designed wayside station building in his Tudor Revival style. Opened in 1844 as Abingdon Road, the station's name was changed to Culham in 1856 when the Abingdon branch from Radley was built. It remains open today but the Brunel building is no longer in railway use. Also, the typical GWR covered footbridge has since been replaced by a more modern structure. The road bridge, out of view on the left, shares Grade II Listing with the station building, being Brunel-designed and also dating from 1844. *Author*

Left Cirencester Town station closed to passengers on 6 April 1964. The 1841-built station building, believed to have been designed by Brunel, is seen here on 10 January 1959 and survives today. *Charles Firminger*

Right This chapter on Brunel's legacy ends with a view of what was arguably his greatest civil engineering work: the Royal Albert Bridge across the River Tamar between Devon and Cornwall built for the financially struggling Cornwall Railway. Brunel was too ill to attend the bridge's opening ceremony on 2 May 1859, although he was transported over it in an open wagon on 4 May. He died four months later at the age of 53. The bridge was officially opened by Queen Victoria's husband, Prince Albert, who also died prematurely some two years later. The bridge is a fitting memorial to the great man because his name is prominently displayed at each end. Here, a goods train travels from Cornwall into Devon on 18 June 1958, some four years before this view would be altered by the arrival of the adjacent road bridge behind Brunel's masterpiece. *Author's collection*

Below Until No 5069 was scrapped in 1962, the great man was celebrated on the longest Castle class nameplate, seen here at Plymouth in 1955. *Photographer unknown/Martin Jenkins collection/Online Transport Archive*

Shipping Services

The GWR was the first mainline railway company to venture into operating shipping services, hardly surprising perhaps since Brunel also designed ships which included three large vessels (such as the preserved SS *Great Britain*) for transatlantic traffic. However, these were never directly owned by the GWR but in 1871 the GWR decided to start operating some localised shipping services, obtaining the necessary parliamentary approval and taking over an existing route between Neyland in Wales and Waterford in Ireland in 1872. Services between Weymouth and the Channel Islands and French ports followed. In 1893 the GWR entered into a joint venture with Ireland's Great Southern & Western Railway called the Fishguard & Rosslare Railways and Harbours Company, with the Welsh terminal being moved to Fishguard in 1906. At one time, the joint venture company owned some 104 miles of Irish track, thus giving the GWR a foothold in Ireland, as well as approximately one mile of track at Fishguard, together with Fishguard and Rosslare harbours. The joint venture company still functions and is now owned by Stena Line and Irish Rail. From 2011-2013, its Deputy Chairman was Dick Fearn, now Chairman of Bluebell Railway plc! Some examples of GWR ships follow.

This vessel is the twin-screw steam ship TSS *Ibex* dating from 1891 and one of three similar ships built for the GWR's Weymouth-Channel Islands route. Despite sinking in 1900 after striking a reef at Guernsey, the TSS *Ibex* was put back into service, and lasted until 1925. During the First World War it was fitted with a rear-mounted gun and sank a U-boat in 1918. *H B Christiansen collection/Online Transport Archive*

Above Triple-screw steam ship TrSS *St Patrick* was one of three ships built for the start of the Fishguard-Rosslare services in 1906. The vessel was scrapped in 1930 after catching fire in the previous year. *H B Christiansen collection/Online Transport Archive*

Below and inset TSS *Sir Walter Raleigh* was built in 1908 and was used by the GWR as a tender at Plymouth where it would sail out to Plymouth Sound to meet a liner temporarily anchored there due to the harbour being too small to accommodate ocean liners.. The tender would then carry passengers and mail back to the GWR's Millbay Docks for onward transportation by train as required, eg to Bristol or Paddington, while the ship continued its journey. TSS *Sir Walter Raleigh* is reckoned to have carried some 170,000 passengers during its 38 years with the GWR. The ticket illustrated was intended for passengers returning from New York to England in April 1912 but this journey never took place because the vessel in question (RMS *Titanic*) never completed its outward voyage.
H B Christiansen collection/Online Transport Archive; Great Western Trust

The Armstrong Brothers

In terms of GWR locomotive design the Armstrong brothers tend to be overlooked when considered alongside the likes of Gooch, Dean and Churchward but both were responsible for some important classes. Joseph Armstrong joined the GWR in 1854, on the amalgamation of his former railway company with the GWR, and was appointed Locomotive Superintendent, Northern Division, based at Stafford Road Works, Wolverhampton. There he worked directly to Gooch at Paddington and was mainly involved with standard gauge locomotives following the acquisition of some as a result of take-overs in the Midlands. Meanwhile Gooch concentrated on broad gauge trains at Swindon Works. In 1864, on Gooch's resignation as principal Locomotive Superintendent and the retirement of J Gibson as Carriage & Wagon superintendent, the roles were merged and Joseph became the GWR's first Locomotive, Carriage & Wagon Superintendent, based at Swindon. The role he vacated at Wolverhampton was then taken over by his younger brother, George, who remained in post until his retirement in 1897, aged 75. He passed away in 1901, but Joseph never reached retirement, dying in harness in 1877. He is probably best remembered for his "Armstrong Standard Goods" and handsome 4-4-0 locomotives but the illustrations which follow depict other significant classes designed by the brothers.

While Joseph Armstrong is probably the better remembered of the two brothers, George can still claim credit for designing some noteworthy small standard gauge tank engines built at Wolverhampton. One such type was the 1901 class of 0-6-0 saddletanks produced from 1881 to 1895. The class numbered 120 and although most were later converted into pannier tanks, some remained as saddletanks, the last of which, No 1925, was not withdrawn until 1951. The locomotive in this photograph is No 1953 built in 1888 and is seen on empty stock duties at Paddington with JW Street, driver of the Cheltenham Flyer on its world speed record run, standing at the front.
Frank Dumbleton collection

Left George Armstrong was also responsible for designing the 517 class, which was particularly significant because the auto-fitted ones were the ancestors of the Collett 48xx (14xx) 0-4-2 tanks. There were 156 members of the 517 class built at Wolverhampton between 1868 and 1885. The engine in this picture is attached to a Churchward auto-trailer, an example of which, No 92 built in 1912, has been restored by the GWS. The train is standing at Abbotsbury station, terminus of a branch from Upwey Junction and Weymouth which closed in 1952. A house has since replaced the station building but the stone goods shed in the distance survives within a farm. The spiked track (flat-bottomed rails fixed directly onto the sleepers) was replaced by GWR bullhead rail in 1937/8. *DWK Jones collection/Online Transport Archive*

Left George Armstrong had considerable autonomy at Wolverhampton and preferred the 0-4-2 wheel arrangement to the 2-4-0 tanks favoured by his brother. Here is Joseph's 455 class 2-4-0 tank No 469, built at Swindon in 1869. The 455 class of 140 locomotives, produced from 1868-1899, originally worked London suburban services including some on the Underground (Metropolitan Railway). As a result they gained the nickname "Metro Tanks" but were mostly displaced on these services by larger tank locomotives and ended up being dispersed widely across the GWR network. *Author's collection*

Left Another of Joseph Armstrong's designs was the 1076 ("Buffalo") class of outside-framed 0-6-0 saddle tanks, 266 being built between 1870 and 1881. This example, No 1610, lasted from 1880 to 1935 and received its pannier tanks in 1927. It was fitted with a spark arresting chimney for working at Didcot's Provender Store (seen in the left background) which contained inflammable animal feed and also at the Government's Central Ordnance Depot where ammunition was stored. *Author's collection*

The Dean Period

William Dean was born in 1840 and was apprenticed to Joseph Armstrong at the GWR's Stafford Road Works in 1855, becoming Joseph's assistant in 1863. In the following year, when Joseph moved to Swindon, Dean became Stafford Road Works manager, responsible to George Armstrong. In 1868, Joseph called Dean to Swindon to become his Chief Assistant and it was inevitable that Dean would get the top job of Locomotive, Carriage and Wagon Superintendent when Joseph died suddenly in 1877. Dean remained in post until his retirement in June 1902 although in latter years he had given increasing responsibility to his assistant, George Jackson Churchward. Dean died three years later aged 65.

During his tenure, Dean had to oversee the conversion of the broad gauge to the standard gauge and this may have restricted his scope for introducing innovative locomotive designs although he can be credited with making engines operate more effectively and efficiently. But it is perhaps in the context of coach development that Dean's expertise came to the fore, with his corridor sets, restaurant and sleeping cars, saloons and the 1897 Royal Train. Some examples of Dean locomotives and rolling stock are depicted in this chapter.

This is one of Dean's 3206 ("Barnum") class engines, No 3210. Built in 1889, there were 20 of this type which were designed for express mixed traffic work. Dean produced several classes of 2-4-0 tender engines and the Barnums were probably the most successful of these, some lasting until 1937. *Harry Luff collection/Online Transport Archive*

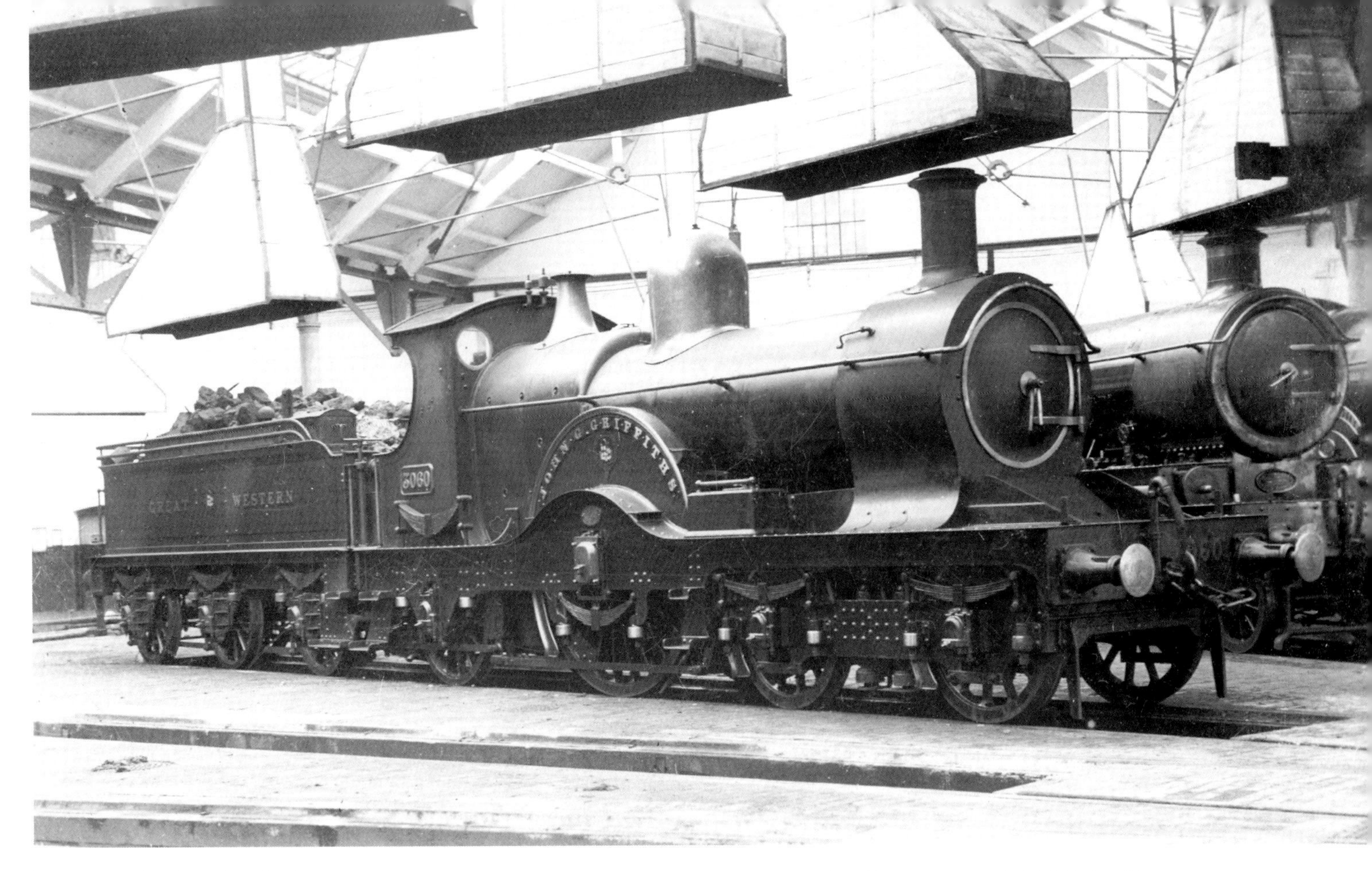

Above Many regard Dean's 4-2-2 Singles (3031 class), at least in their original condition, as one of the most handsome locomotive types on the GWR, if not in Great Britain. The class was constructed at Swindon between 1891 and 1899 and the first eight were built as Broad Gauge "convertibles". In fact, the initial thirty were originally 2-2-2s but these received front bogies after a derailment in 1893 which was blamed on excessive weight being carried on the front axle. This example, No 3060 *John G Griffiths*, dates from 1895 and was originally named *Warlock*, but was re-named after Mr Griffiths (a GWR director) in March 1908. No 3060 received a new boiler (which arguably marred its appearance) in June 1911 so the photograph would have been taken between these two dates. The name was transferred to another engine (Bulldog class No 3412) in March 1914 and No 3060 was withdrawn in March 1915. *Harry Luff collection/Online Transport Archive*

Left No original Dean Singles survive, although a new build has been mooted, but a non-working replica of No 3041, *The Queen*, a former Royal train locomotive, was built in 1982 for Tussauds' Railway and Royalty Exhibition at Windsor & Eton Central station. The locomotive was paired with a tender and attached to two carriages (one originally from the 1897 Royal Train) but the exhibition subsequently closed and only the engine (minus its tender and carriages) remains at Windsor station. *Author*

Above Dean's Aberdare 2600 class 2-6-0s consisted of 80 engines built between 1900 and 1907 and were intended for hauling coal trains between Aberdare and Swindon, hence their nickname. Their lives were prolonged by the Second World War, twelve passing to BR in 1948. This photograph depicts No 2640 in Whitnash cutting south of Leamington Spa in 1926, with a train consisting mainly of Portland cement/lime vans from Greaves Siding at Harbury. The milepost marked 104 is misleading because it appears not to have been altered since the Great Western/Great Central Joint line was opened in 1906, avoiding the need to reach Birmingham via Didcot and Oxford and shaving some 18 miles off the route. *Stanley Eades/Online Transport Archive*

Left The Aberdares became extinct in 1949 and this view from the previous year depicts No 2620 passing the HMV factory at Hayes, Middlesex on a down freight. Behind the tender is a wagon previously belonging to the West Cannock Colliery Company, Staffordshire, which was absorbed by the newly-formed National Coal Board in 1946. *David Cable/Online Transport Archive*

Above and right Probably the most successful Dean type of locomotive was the 2301 Standard Goods class 0-6-0s, built from 1883 to 1899. Their reputation was so high that large numbers were requisitioned for use in continental Europe during the First World War and, amazingly considering their age, also for the Second World War, including twenty-four which had already served abroad in the previous war. The last survivor of this much loved class known as "Dean Goods", No 2538, was withdrawn in May 1957 but in the previous year No 2516, built in 1897, had been set aside for preservation and is currently on static display at Steam Museum, Swindon. These pictures show an unidentified example at Penmaenpool attached to the Shrewsbury Divisional Engineer's ex-Bristol & Exeter Railway saloon in April 1935 and No 2516 outside Swindon Works on 5 May 1958, sandwiched between preserved No 4003 *Lode Star* and its tender. *C E R Sherrington/Frank Dumbleton collection; Jim Oatway*

Dean Goods No 2538 was not, however, the last working Dean locomotive when it was withdrawn in 1957. It was still possible to go to Wales as late as 1960 to see a Dean locomotive in action. Back in 1894, Dean's Duke class 4-4-0s entered service, all with curved outside frames, while in 1898 the first of Dean's heavier Bulldog class 4-4-0s emerged, later ones having straight-topped frames. For many years the Cambrian lines were subject to weight limitations which precluded the use of Bulldogs while allowing Dukes. However, by the early 1930s the Dukes were wearing out, primarily because their curved frames were weaker than those Bulldogs which had straight frames. To overcome the problem, the GWR decided to rebuild thirty Dukes (the first was a prototype) by using Bulldog straight frames. This hybrid type, which satisfied the Cambrian restrictions, was initially named after Earls, following the precedent set by the Dukes, but following protests about the Earls' names being placed on these antiquated-looking engines, the plates were transferred to a batch of new Castle class 4-6-0s. These 4-4-0s then became known as "Dukedogs", reflecting their origins. The last Dukedog to remain in service was No 9017 which was allocated the name *Earl of Berkeley* but never carried it. This locomotive, which was created in 1938, consisted of the top half of Duke No 3282 *Chepstow Castle* dating from 1899 and the lower half of Bulldog No 3425, built in 1906. No 9017 was withdrawn in October 1960 and dispatched to Oswestry Works pending a successful preservation appeal, to which I donated 15 shillings of my pocket money. I was then was able to see No 9017 at Old Oak Common MPD as it made its way in steam on 14/15 February 1962 to the Bluebell Railway in Sussex (where it still resides). The picture (above) taken on 24 September 1960 shows No 9017 piloting Collett 2-6-0 No 7330 on the Talyllyn Railway AGM Special near Cemmes Road, Powys, on the now closed former Newtown and Machynlleth Railway. *Alan Sainty collection*

Left The 157 class of 2-2-2 locomotives (Nos 157-166) dating from 1878-9 are regarded as one of Dean's most attractive types. They were designed for express work but most were withdrawn in 1903-6 following the introduction of more powerful classes to haul heavier trains, although the last was not withdrawn until 1914. No 157 is pictured on a down express at Acton. *Great Western Trust*

Below Dean's Bulldog class of mixed traffic 4-4-0s was introduced in 1899 and the first twenty-one (Nos 3332-3352) were built with curved-topped outside frames. An example from this batch, No 3334 *Tavy*, is seen at Appleford on the Didcot-Oxford line. The locomotive entered service in 1900 as No 3346, being renumbered in 1912. As evidenced here, these early Bulldogs carried an oval combined number and nameplate on their cabsides. No 3334 was withdrawn in 1930 as the newly introduced Collett Hall class 4-6-0s started to take over many of the Bulldogs' duties. *Great Western Trust*

Above Utilising an unusual wheel arrangement for the GWR, Dean produced 31 2-4-2 tanks of the 3600 class between 1900 and 1903. Nicknamed "Birdcages" due to their spacious cabs, these locomotives were designed for fast suburban traffic and this example, No 3611, is working a London local service. All were withdrawn in 1930-34 following the arrival of more powerful prairie tanks. *Author's collection*

Right Turning now to Dean coaching stock, this picture and the three opposite depict the body of a unique vehicle which is currently a chalet in West Wales in which my family and I spent a holiday during August 1995. *Author*

The coach body is a composite Family Saloon, No 247 (later No 9043) with a "Royal Clerestory" roof, ie sloping ends, built in 1892. An 8-wheeler some 38ft long, it consists of a first class open saloon from which a side corridor leads to the lavatory/WC cubicle and a first class compartment, then opening up into a servants' compartment and a luggage/guard's compartment. One particularly unusual feature is that it has observation windows inserted in one end enabling passengers to enjoy the view from two swivel armchairs. *Author-all*

Above Two Dean-period four-wheelers are seen on the Cleobury, Mortimer & Ditton Priors Light Railway in Shropshire, attached to one of that Railway's two former saddletanks. In 1922, the Light Railway was absorbed into the GWR which converted the engines into pannier tanks and numbered them 28 and 29, arguably inspiring the creation of Collett's later 1366 class (see page 66). The line opened in 1908 but passenger services ceased in 1938 although, due to the location of an armaments depot at Ditton Priors, the line itself remained open until 1960. *Author's collection*

Below 1897 was Queen Victoria's Diamond Jubilee marking sixty years on the Throne and the GWR decided to provide her with a new Royal Train. This consisted of six corridor carriages comprising two full brakes, one Officials' Saloon (No 233), a reconstructed Queen's Saloon from the previous Royal Train, one Attendants Saloon (No 234) and one First Saloon. Here is the Royal Train carrying the Monarch from Windsor to Paddington in 1897 passing through Castle Hill and Ealing Dene station (renamed West Ealing in 1899) behind a Dean Single (probably No 3041 *The Queen*). The second carriage, No 234, and the fourth, No 233, both survive today. The building with a tower in the right corner of the picture is the Drayton Court Hotel which opened in 1894 and where, in 1914, Ho Chi Minh (the subsequently famous Vietnamese leader) worked in the kitchens! *E J Bedford*

On withdrawal, the bodies of Nos 233 and 234 were sold and placed on a caravan/camping site at Aberporth in West Wales. I spent a weekend in No 233 in 1973. The body was subsequently sold to Tussauds for their Railways and Royalty Exhibition at Windsor (it is currently in Steam Museum, Swindon) while No 234 is now privately preserved at St Germans in Cornwall. Both bodies have been mounted on BR Mk1 coach chassis. These pictures depict the exterior and interior of No 233 at Windsor and the interior of No 234 when at Aberporth. *Author-all*

Above This picture depicts two Dean coaches attached to an engine which was operated by the GWR from 1908 and subsequently "Greatwesternised". The locomotive is ex-Port Talbot Railway & Docks Company 0-6-0 tank No 26 (later GWR No 813) dating from 1901, photographed on 29 April 2017 while on a visit from the Severn Valley Railway to celebrate 50 years of the GWS at its Didcot home. No 813 is seen running alongside Didcot's mixed gauge track hauling Dean clerestory No 1941 dating from 1901 and Brake Third No 416 (ex-Camping Coach No 9940) built in 1891. The locomotive owes its survival to the fact that, following withdrawal by the GWR in 1933, it was sold for colliery use in north east England where it remained until purchased by the GWR 813 Preservation Fund in 1967. *Frank Dumbleton*

Centre and Lower The exterior of No 1941 reveals the splendour of the GWR's intricate coach livery around the turn of the 20th century. The carriage was designed to carry 80 third class passengers in eight compartments, with the clerestory roof providing increased spaciousness and light, as evidenced in this interior view, compared with elliptical-roofed stock. No 1941 retains its original body and chassis and survived because it was converted to Departmental use rather than being scrapped on withdrawal from passenger service. The vehicle was purchased in 1968 when found languishing at Cardiff. *Nigel Hunt; Frank Dumbleton*

Above This is a view of St Ives station and yard around 1930 with a selection of wagons and vans belonging to various railway companies. The GWR carriages consist of two Dean clerestory vehicles and a Collett coach. *William Dighton/ Author's collection*

Right Here is an assortment of rolling stock photographed from a passing train also around 1930. Sandwiched between a cattle wagon and a horse box is a Dean four-wheeled coach, with a Churchward auto-trailer on the end. *C E R Sherrington/Frank Dumbleton collection*

We shall end this review of Dean passenger carriages with some photographs of my third class family saloon No 2511. Built at Swindon in 1894 and withdrawn in October 1937, the body of No 2511 was then transported to Purley on Thames, becoming 10 River Gardens. Requiring removal due to site redevelopment, the body was acquired by me and taken to Didcot Railway Centre on 16 April 1972. In the following year, I was able to purchase a contemporary GWR six-wheeled chassis (ex-DW 109), on which the body was placed. The carriage is remarkable because, in addition to the exterior requiring only minimal attention, most of the interior is GWR original, albeit the upholstery is from its final refit around 1930 and the mahogany panelling from around 1910 when second class was abolished and third class upgraded. *Frank Dumbleton; Author*

Right The following seven pictures depict some examples of GWR style which survived within the interior of my Dean Family Saloon No 2511. We start with one of the Photochrom coloured pictures, appropriately featuring Brunel's Clifton Suspension Bridge built after his death.

Right No 2511 seems to have been in public service until its withdrawal because beneath domestic mirrors in the tops of the four exterior doors were Restaurant Car Services notices bearing the 1930s GWR roundel motif. Beneath the sign is an early style blind. The carriage boasted a complete set of these. *Frank Dumbleton-both*

Left and above These third class family vehicles comprised two saloons separated by two cubicles, one a lavatory (wash room) and the other a WC. There is a water tank in the roof which supplies the lavatory hand basin and WC, the water being drawn down by using handles such as this one, i.e. there are no taps or cistern, as is evident in this picture of the handbasin. The water enters the basin from beneath the overhanging lip behind the plug hole.

Below The brass window sign is self-explanatory. The two saloons were latterly designated A and B, suggesting that, whereas originally one group/family would probably hire the complete carriage, in later life, as usage reduced, two families/groups could hire it, assuming they were going to the same destination! *Frank Dumbleton-all*

Above The luggage racks above the seats on either side of the leaf table are weaker because, unlike the transverse ones, the ends are not secured to the walls.

Below Behind one of the original double pictures above the transverse seats, this paper notice from the First World War was discovered. *Frank Dumbleton-both*

GREAT WESTERN RAILWAY.

Defence of the Realm (Consolidation) Regulations, 1914.

OBLIGATION ON PASSENGERS TO KEEP BLINDS OF COMPARTMENTS LOWERED AFTER SUNSET.

Extract from Clause II of Order of Secretary of State, dated December 15th, 1915:—

"Passengers in railway carriages which are provided with blinds MUST keep the blinds lowered so as to cover the windows. The blinds may be lifted in case of necessity when the train is at a standstill at a station, but if lifted they must be lowered again before the train starts."

Road Transport Services

The GWR was the first standard gauge railway company in Great Britain to operate motor bus services. The decision to enter this market was made because the Company was under pressure to build a light railway into deepest Cornwall from Helston, terminus of the branch line from Gwinear Road, and wished to test potential passenger traffic before incurring the costs of constructing a line. Thus, on 17 August 1903 the GWR started its first bus route, operating between Helston Station and The Lizard, and this proved to be very popular. The Company quickly recognised that, in addition to saving construction costs in building new railway lines, particularly in sparsely populated areas, bus operation could also provide feeder services to bring prospective passengers to its railway stations and, later on, helping to deter competition from other bus operators.

Following the success of the inaugural service, the GWR wasted no time in creating new bus routes. On 31 October 1903, the Company began services between Penzance and Marazion and several more were introduced in the West Country in 1904. Also in that year the GWR started bus operation in other parts of the system, for example between Slough and Beaconsfield from 1 March, Slough and Windsor from 18 July, in the Wrexham area from 11 October and Wolverhampton to Bridgnorth from 7 November. There was no stopping the GWR and in due course it had the largest bus fleet of any of the railway companies. However, bus companies voiced their concern at what they perceived as unfair competition and in 1928 an Act was passed regulating bus operation by railway companies. This paved the way to the creation of "railway associated" bus companies and by 1933 the GWR abandoned bus services, having obtained significant shareholdings in bus companies such as Western National, Devon General and Thames Valley, ensuring that railway feeder services would continue. On the other hand, the Company continued operating its lucrative road freight services for the remainder of its existence and amassed a sizable fleet.

Left Original GWR omnibus No 1268, a 1927 Guy FBB 32-seater with GWR-designed bodywork by Vickers of Crayford, stands outside the Top House Inn at The Lizard, terminus of the first bus service, in August 2013, celebrating the 110th Anniversary. No 1268 was transferred to the Western National Omnibus Company, in which the GWR held a 50% stake, in 1929 and owes its survival to being converted into a caravan and then becoming a holiday chalet in Cornwall. It is now part of the Thames Valley and Great Western Omnibus Trust collection based at Fifield near Maidenhead. *Amyas Crump*

Left The GWR had a large fleet of vans and lorries, an example of which is this 1930s Scammell "Mechanical Horse" with flatbed trailer, registered as BNX 833. *John Herting/Online Transport Archive*

Above This view of Didcot station forecourt in 1925 features GWR omnibus No 872 (YK 2838), a new AEC vehicle with Buckingham 18-seater bodywork. The station buildings seen in these pictures dated from 1892 and were replaced in 1985.

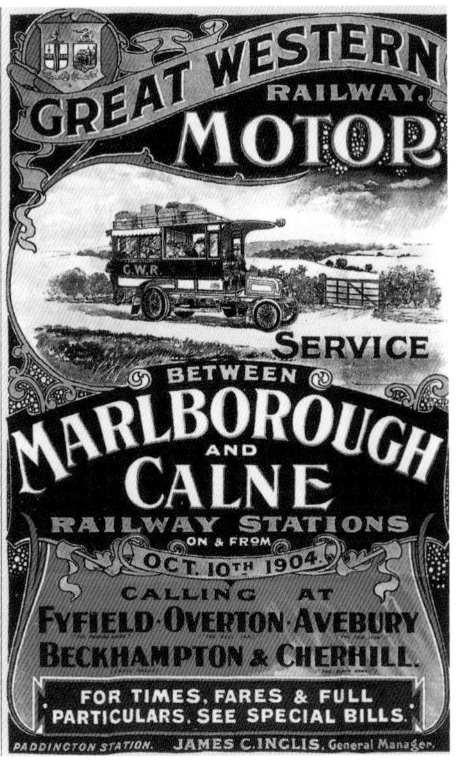

Left Here is a 1904 leaflet advertising a new GWR motor bus service in Wiltshire.

Below A service to Holyport waits at Maidenhead. *Frank Dumbleton collection; Great Western Trust; E.N. Osborne/Martin Jenkins collection*

The Churchward Revolution

George Jackson Churchward was a pioneering genius and undoubtedly one of Britain's greatest railway designers/engineers. Born in 1857 he began his railway career with the South Devon Railway in 1873 and when this Company was absorbed by the GWR in 1876 he moved to Swindon. In 1885 he was appointed Carriage Works Manager and in 1895 he was promoted to Locomotive Works Manager. As William Dean's health began to deteriorate Churchward became Dean's Chief Assistant in 1897, taking over as Locomotive, Carriage and Wagon Superintendent on Dean's retirement in May 1902. Over the final years of Dean's reign, Churchward was already developing ideas that would revolutionise locomotive design and bring the GWR firmly into the 20th century. His concepts, which were partly influenced by American and French practice, included the adoption of high pressure domeless tapered boilers, Belpaire fireboxes, superheaters, long travel valves and maximum standardisation of parts linked with the introduction of a limited number of standard locomotive types. These influential designs formed the basis of later engines developed by his successors, Collett and Hawksworth, which lasted to the end of WR steam. Indeed several of his original locomotive types survived in service into 1964 and a handful into 1965.

Churchward retired in 1922, his post having been changed to Chief Mechanical Engineer (CME) in 1916, and died tragically in 1933 after being struck by an express train while checking some trackwork close to his home. Pictures of his major designs now follow.

Churchward is not normally associated with outside-framed locomotives of Victorian appearance but the City and Flower classes of express 4-4-0s emerged under his tenure between 1903 and 1908 for reasons which are not obvious, particularly since his modern-looking County 4-4-0s were built largely over this period. The construction of further Bulldog class outside-framed 4-4-0s also continued, right up to 1910, but that could be justified because Churchward had not introduced his general purpose 2-6-0s until then. Withdrawn in 1931, preserved City class No 3440 *City of Truro*, alleged speed record-holder, is seen here at Swindon on 13 April 1958.
Neil Davenport/Online Transport Archive

Above In contrast, Churchward's design style is far more associated with more modern objects of beauty such as this two-cylinder Saint class locomotive from 1905, No 175 *Viscount Churchill*, the name subsequently being transferred to Castle locomotive No 111 in 1924 following the demise of *The Great Bear* (see page 50). *Viscount Churchill* joined the GWR Board in 1905 and was the Company's Chairman from 1908 until his death in 1934. *Author's collection*

Right The GWR's first express passenger 4-6-0, No 100, soon to be named *William Dean*, emerged from Swindon in February 1902 and so, by three months, is technically a Dean locomotive but clearly designed by Churchward. Seen here leaving Paddington around 1912 just before being re-numbered 2900, the locomotive then became the doyen of the Saint series of 77 locomotives built between 1903 and 1913 although the remainder of the class were actually based on the second prototype, No 98 (later No 2998) completed in March 1903. The failure to preserve the last survivor of this iconic class following withdrawal in October 1953 has long been regarded as a major omission, given the type's ground-breaking design. However, the GWS has rectified this aberration by creating a new Saint locomotive, No 2999 *Lady of Legend*, taking advantage of the GWR's standardisation policy introduced by Churchward (ie mainly using parts from other locomotives). No 2999's design is based on the ten "Ladies" as built in 1906 in their original condition without curved drop-ends to the frames. *Great Western Trust*

Here are two Saint class 4-6-0 locomotives, the first having curved drop-ends to the frames and the second having the original style frames as fitted to the "Ladies" when built. No 2981 *Ivanhoe*, seen at Shrewsbury, was one of several named after characters in Sir Walter Scott's novels. It was originally constructed in 1905 as an Atlantic (4-4-2) because Churchward wished to carry out comparative trials with three French compound locomotives imported by the GWR which were also 4-4-2s. In the end Churchward opted for 4-6-0s and also decided that compounding made no difference to performance. No 2981 was rebuilt as a 4-6-0 in 1912 and lasted until 1951. No 2902 *Lady of the Lake*, pictured at Paddington's Platform 1, was built in 1906 as a 4-6-0 and was withdrawn in 1949. *Author's collection-both*

The next prototype of a modern Churchward class emerged from Swindon in June 1903 and was arguably the most successful because of its longevity in largely unrebuilt form, due to being unrivalled. However, this achievement and the fact that the pioneer, No 97 (which became No 2800 in 1912) (*above*), was Britain's first 2-8-0 locomotive is generally overlooked simply because it was an unglamorous heavy freight type. Fortunately, BR realised its importance by saving the most original surviving one, No 2818, after nearly 58 years of hard work. In fact several members of the 2800 class clocked up similar lengths of service, some lasting until 1964. Collett went on to upgrade Churchward's design, producing the 2884 class with side window cab. However, the example depicted below at Old Oak Common on 20 September 1947 still has the wartime blackout sliding panel in place of glass. The engine is No 3831, temporarily renumbered 4857 while it was fitted for oil burning, a short-lived unsuccessful experiment. *Frank Dumbleton collection; Author's collection*

Following on from No 97 was No 99 dating from September 1903. This locomotive was the original large Prairie tank, which formed the basis of several similar-looking classes built up to 1949 (ie into BR days), many of which lasted until the official end of WR steam on 31 December 1965. No 99 underwent various modifications over the years as well as changes of identity, becoming No 3100 in 1912, No 5100 in 1929 and finally No 8100 in 1938. Examples of variants follow on this and the opposite page.

Above On the last day of passenger services on the Moretonhampstead branch, 28 February 1959, the addition of a fourth carriage in the afternoon was considered too onerous for 0-4-2 tank No 1466 after it had set an embankment alight. Consequently, the 2.15pm from Newton Abbot was hauled by large prairie tank No 4117, seen crossing the River Wrey on its way to Lustleigh. *Les Folkard/Online Transport Archive*

Opposite upper Seventy slightly more powerful large Prairies were built for London commuter traffic. This was the 6100 class, represented in this view at Basingstoke on 30 May 1964 by No 6136. Built in 1932 (therefore technically a Collett designed engine), it is seen in its final livery of unlined green and it lasted to the end of WR steam. *Neil Davenport/Online Transport Archive)*

Opposite lower No 4174, photographed at Dawlish in October 1962, was a Collett adaptation of Churchward's original design which was built as late as 1949, i.e. under BR auspices. *Alan Sainty collection*

6136

4174

Churchward's next prototype gave rise to a somewhat short-lived tender engine class and tank engine variant. No 3473 (later No 3800) *County of Middlesex* was an outside-cylindered 4-4-0 with 6ft 8½in driving wheels completed in May 1904, becoming the doyen of the 40-strong County class, built up to 1912. The engines followed Churchward's standardisation policy for modern locomotives and were specifically designed for express work. They were very fast machines but the amount of power generated, combined with this wheel arrangement, made them somewhat "front-heavy", resulting in their acquiring a reputation for being "rough riders". Nonetheless, this was a successful locomotive type, yet they were withdrawn between 1930 and 1933 which was much the same time as all the other large-wheeled 4-4-0s, these being the antiquated-looking outside-framed types. The reason seems to be that, as they had been replaced on express work by 4-6-0s, the secondary duties to which they had been demoted could be covered by more versatile locomotives such as Halls and Moguls. The 4-4-2 County Tank version with slightly smaller boiler, pioneered by No 2221 in September 1905 and designed for London commuter traffic, suffered the same fate, being replaced by Collett's more effective 6100 class of 2-6-2 tanks. The County tanks, which numbered 30, were all withdrawn between 1931 and 1935. No County 4-4-0s or 4-4-2 tanks survive but construction of a new one of each type using some parts from other GWR classes is a future possibility.

This page No 3822 *County of Brecon* lingers on the approaches to Old Oak Common MPD around 1930. *William Dighton/Author's collection*

Opposite upper Both No 3822 and this example, No 3821 *County of Bedford* seen on a freight train, belonged to the final batch from 1911-12 and were built with superheaters and curved drop ends to the footplating. *Author's collection*

Opposite lower A County Tank waits at Didcot with a suburban train to Paddington. The photograph was taken between 1921, when removal of the semi-circular fittings on the top of the tanks associated with two-way water scoops began and 1932 when Didcot engine shed, visible on the right, was rebuilt.
C E R Sherrington/Frank Dumbleton collection

We now come to small Prairie 2-6-2 tanks. The first, No 4400, was built in October 1904, the first of eleven examples of this type designed for hilly branch lines, such as the Princetown line across Dartmoor. Withdrawal occurred between 1949 and 1955. Much better known were the successor 4500 class which had larger wheels. This type numbered 75 engines, with construction ceasing in 1924. Collett then modified Churchward's design by fitting larger water tanks, thereby increasing their range. This type was called the 4575 class and the first one entered service in February 1927.

Above This view at Ashley Hill, on the Bristol Parkway-Temple Meads line, depicts the type in its earliest incarnation. This included a straight-back bunker, works plate in the centre of the smokebox saddle and the absence of both a superheater and front end struts. Carrying its original number of 2163 this 1906-built locomotive was renumbered 4502 in 1912 and withdrawn in 1954. It belonged to the final batch of locomotives to be built at Wolverhampton (Stafford Road) Works. *Great Western Trust*

Opposite upper Against the backdrop of two Churchward Toplight carriages, one of which bears a Paddington-Exeter-Plymouth roofboard, No 5522 stands in Taunton station with a local train which includes a cattle wagon. This locomotive represents Collett's development of Churchward's original small prairie type with larger tanks. *Author's collection*

Lower Another Collett small prairie, No 5541, stands under a typical GWR covered footbridge as it occupies the centre road at Tavistock with a pick-up freight on 16 June 1962. Tavistock was situated on the GWR's Plymouth-Launceston branch which closed to passengers in 1962 and to freight in 1964.
Great Western Trust

5541

If Churchward's two-cylinder locomotive No 100 created a sensation in the railway world in 1902 (see page 39) his 4-cylinder locomotive No 40 caused an earthquake. Subsequently named *North Star*, No 40 emerged from Swindon in April 1906 as a 4-4-2, again for the purpose of undergoing comparison trials with the three French 4-cylinder compound locomotives imported in 1903-5. Churchward was looking to design a fast express engine which was also powerful enough to take heavy trains over the Devon Banks and decided that four cylinder engines were needed and that 4-6-0s provided better adhesion than 4-4-2s. No 40 (becoming No 4000 from 1912) was converted to the 4-6-0 wheel arrangement in November 1909 and all the production Stars built from 1907 to 1923 were 4-6-0s. Fifteen were later rebuilt by Collett to become members of the Castle class but several of the unrebuilt ones lasted into the 1950s, including No 4003 *Lode Star* dating from February 1907 which was set aside for preservation following its withdrawal in July 1951 (see opposite) and is currently at the National Railway Museum, York.

This page In its earliest incarnation dating from1907, No 4006 *Red Star* is seen with brass moulding around its splashers, a feature which was removed in 1914 from Stars and other classes to assist with the War effort. No 4006 is also carrying a works plate on its centre splasher. These plates were discontinued in 1911. In this view, the locomotive's safety valve cover is obscured by drifting steam from the chimney. *Author's collection*

Opposite The picture of Dean Goods No 2516 at Swindon Works on page 23 provides a glimpse of the preserved Star class 4-6-0 No 4003 *Lode Star*. Here is the complete engine. *Below*, an unidentified Star is pictured on the Paddington-Birmingham line in Whitnash cutting near Leamington Spa in 1926.
Jim Oatway; Stanley Eades/Online Transport Archive

LODE STAR
4003

In February 1908, Churchward produced a one-off enigma, No 111 *The Great Bear*. It was Britain's first 4-6-2 and the ensuing publicity which this attracted was arguably the only reason for its being built. The locomotive became the GWR's flagship until this mantle was taken over by the first Collett Castle, *Caerphilly Castle*, quickly followed by Collett's *King George V*. However, it has been said that the main reason for No 111's construction was to trial a larger type of boiler, indicating that this was a case of forward thinking by Churchward in anticipation of future heavier trains. In any event, the engine's fame was not matched by its performance which was mediocre. Furthermore, due to its axle loading it was restricted to the London-Bristol mainline which was another disadvantage. As soon as Churchward retired, Collett withdrew it (ostensibly because it was due for heavy repairs) and converted it into a Castle class 4-6-0, No 111 *Viscount Churchill*, although scarcely anything of the original engine was used. In its revised form, No 111 lasted until July 1953.

This page Despite its operational shortcomings, the locomotive looks impressive as it heads a down express composed of Churchward 70ft Dreadnought carriages dating from 1904-7, so named after a type of battleship because of their huge size (70ft long by 9ft 6ins wide). One Dreadnought coach survives and awaits restoration at Didcot Railway Centre. *Frank Dumbleton collection*

It would be difficult to find a greater contrast between two Churchward types than the prestigious first British pacific seen opposite and the 1361 class of dock shunter depicted on this page. However, although attributed to Churchward as Locomotive Superintendent the designer was actually Harold Holcroft, the GWR's Chief Draughtsman, who simply updated GWR rebuilds of ex-Cornwall Minerals Railway engines following that Company's acquisition by the GWR in 1896. These rebuilds became the 1392 class and (*above*) No 1394 was photographed standing with No 1395 sometime before its withdrawal in 1933. The similarity between this engine and (*left*) No 1361, photographed at Weymouth Dock on 22 April 1960 near the end of a ten-week stint there, is obvious. The 1361 class of five locomotives were built in 1910, becoming the GWR's final saddletank type because contemporary GWR policy was to fit square-topped Belpaire fireboxes to saddle tank engines and convert them into pannier tanks. However, the 1361 class had round-topped fireboxes like their predecessors. One example, No 1363, survives, having been purchased by the GWS, and is based at Didcot. *Author's collection; Alan Sainty collection*

Another type introduced in 1910 was the 4200 class of 2-8-0 tanks designed for short-haul mineral trains. The class consisted of 205 locomotives built between 1910 and 1930 which were numbered in the 42XX and 52XX series. However, some renumbering took place due to the fact that 54 were rebuilt by Collett into 2-8-2 tanks between 1934 and 1937, becoming the 7200 class, the extra length enabling a larger coal bunker to be fitted.

Left This example, No 4241, pictured at Duffryn Yard MPD in July 1962, was built in 1914, withdrawn in April 1964 and never received outside steam pipes.

Below Displaying its huge bunker, 2-8-2 tank No 7226, seen at Cardiff General in the company of No 5099 *Compton Castle*, was rebuilt in 1935 from 2-8-0 tank No 5261. *Alan Sainty collection-both*

Whereas Dean's maid of all work was his Standard Goods 0-6-0 type Churchward's equivalent was his 4300 class "Mogul" 2-6-0. This was a tender version of one of his large "Prairie Tank" types, in this case the 3150 class which emerged in 1906 as a variation of the 3100 class with a larger boiler. Churchward's Moguls were a mixed traffic type intended to supersede Dean's 4-4-0s and 342 were produced virtually continuously from 1911 to 1932, including twenty of the Collett version with side window cab, Nos 9300-9319 (later renumbered 7322-7341). One hundred were withdrawn in 1936-9 so that their wheels and motion could be used for two new Collett 4-6-0 classes, the 80 Granges and the first 20 Manors (the Second World War terminated this programme). Some Moguls lasted into 1964 including two which were fortunate to be sent to Woodhams scrapyard and have since been restored to running order. These are Churchward No 5322 which was one of eleven that served abroad during the First World War and is now at Didcot and Collett No 7325 (ex- No 9303) with side window cab which is on the Severn Valley Railway.

This page This unidentified 4300 class 2-6-0 was photographed on a passenger working at Penzance around 1930. *William Dighton/Author's collection*

Churchward/Collett 4300 class Moguls were used indiscriminately on passenger or freight duties and this latter traffic is featured on this page.

Above In this August 1962 view at Towyn (Tywyn) in Wales, shunting is being performed by Mogul No 6353. When this 1923-built locomotive was withdrawn in 1963 it was one of relatively few class members still retaining inside steam pipes. *Jim Oatway*

Left An unidentified Mogul enters Leamington Spa station in 1926. The advertisement on the side of the building refers to a large department store in Bath Street founded in 1840. *Stanley Eades/ Online Transport Archive*

100,000. Est. 178. 9/44. S.

(5073 G)

G.W.R.

Via **LEAMINGTON** AND **L.M. & S.**

Churchward's final locomotive design was his powerful 4700 class 2-8-0s which numbered nine and were designed for heavy mixed traffic work beyond the ability of his 4300 class 2-6-0s. No 4700 was completed in May 1919 and fitted with a larger boiler in May 1921. Following that change, eight further locomotives were built in 1922-3, all with the larger boiler and, like the prototype, with 5ft 8in driving wheels. They were however route restricted and Collett decided that his new Hall class (see page 60) was a better option, being more versatile and capable of handling most of the larger type's work. The main role of the 4700 class was to haul fast overnight freight trains but from the outset they were also used on passenger trains, in particular summer relief expresses. None of the original nine locomotives (Nos 4700-4708) survives despite withdrawal not taking place until June 1962-May 1964 but the GWS is creating another one (No 4709) using a combination of parts from "Barry hulks" and new material. Construction is being undertaken at the Llangollen Railway Works.

This page No 4700 prepares to leave Newton Abbot with a Southern Region excursion train in May 1962. *Jim Oatway*

The GWR was a major user of steam powered carriages (rail motors) and Churchward introduced these in 1903, with 99 being built up to 1908. The Company had been concerned about the competition from buses and tramways and saw railmotors, which could be driven from either end with a guard issuing tickets in the vehicle, as a means of simplifying and improving local rail services. However, the railmotors were victims of their own success because the increased passenger traffic that they generated could not always be accommodated within a single vehicle and the small vertically-mounted steam engine within the carriage was not sufficiently powerful to haul a trailer unless the line was particularly flat. It was also difficult to keep the passenger section clean because of the need to service them in steam depots. These problems were quickly identified because, although a few steam railmotors lasted until 1935 (albeit the first was withdrawn in 1914), a start was made as early as 1905 to convert some locomotives (notably the Armstrong 517 class of 0-4-2s) to operate on a "push and pull" basis in conjunction with a specially adapted "auto-coach" containing a driving vestibule at the rear. In 1970, the GWS obtained a former steam railmotor (No 93 built in 1908 and withdrawn in November 1934) which had been converted into trailer No 212 and was latterly used as an office. With the construction of a replica boiler to fit inside the carriage, No 93 is a working steam railmotor once again.

This page No 93 is seen giving rides at Old Oak Common Open Day on 2 September 2017, an event signifying the closure of the depot after 111 years. The railmotor has the "Toplight" style of smaller upper windows, a characteristic of much of Churchward's coach stock. *Frank Dumbleton*

Left This is the restored interior of No 93 looking towards the driving vestibule. The seats, apart from the benches, have reversible backs similar to those on traditional tramcars. In fact the metal frames were obtained from withdrawn tramcars in Australia which had been manufactured by the same Slough firm that had supplied similar seats to the GWR for its railmotors! *Frank Dumbleton*

Below A typical example of Churchward's carriage design is provided by Churchward "Toplight" corridor third No 8930, seen here on the Severn Valley Railway in March 2012. This vehicle was built in 1915 and is carrying 1922 Collett livery which brought a return to chocolate and cream after the discontinuation of crimson lake exemplified by railmotor No 93 opposite. *Hugh Llewelyn/Wiki Commons ref 6901712218*

The Collett Era

Charles Benjamin Collett joined the GWR in 1893 as a draughtsman at Swindon, rising to become Works Manager in 1912 and Churchward's deputy in 1919. He was appointed CME on Churchward's retirement in 1922 (a position he retained until the age of 70 in 1941) and quickly found himself having to deal with issues arising from the Grouping. In particular he had to decide what to do with the masses of locomotives and rolling stock inherited from the Welsh railway companies, but he still found time to design new classes of locomotives. In the Churchward chapter of this book some of the Collett adaptations of Churchward locomotives were pictured but the locomotives covered in this Collett chapter are new classes attributed to Collett as designer even though some are nevertheless inspired by Churchward's work. Starting with his famous Castle class, Collett considered that an engine more powerful than the Star class while ensuring fairly wide route availability was necessary. His 4-6-0 therefore had a larger boiler and increased cylinder diameter, making this arguably Britain's most powerful locomotive. The GWR emphasised this when the prototype, No 4073 *Caerphilly Castle*, was exhibited with the LNER's Gresley Pacific, *Flying Scotsman*, at the British Empire Exhibition at Wembley in 1924. The LNER naturally disputed this and comparative trials were arranged in 1925 when No 4079 *Pendennis Castle* unquestionably outshone its LNER rival and was then exhibited beside *Flying Scotsman* in the 1925 Wembley Exhibition (to add justifiable insult to injury!).

This page No 4073 *Caerphilly Castle*, now preserved at the Steam Museum, Swindon, entered service on 11 August 1923 and this view taken shortly after captures the locomotive storming out of Paddington. The diagonal guttering on the cab roof was unique to No 4073. *Author's collection*

Opposite upper No 5005 *Manorbier Castle*, pictured near Old Oak Common in the late 1920s, was built in June 1927 and is attached to a 3,500 gallon tender which was standard for Castles at this time. This engine went on to be mutilated, along with King class 4-6-0 No 6014 (see page 63), for a streamlining experiment apparently forced on Collett by GWR management. *William Dighton/Author's collection*

Opposite lower The Castle class continued to be built into BR days, the last one, No 7037 *Swindon*, being completed in August 1950 and running without nameplates until named by HRH Princess Elizabeth (now HM The Queen) on 15 November 1950. On the same day she drove Star class locomotive No 4057 *Princess Elizabeth*, following in the footsteps of her grandfather, King George V, who drove No 4082 *Windsor Castle* at Swindon in 1924. Here is No 7037 *Swindon*, adorned with the GWR crest on its centre splasher, outside Old Oak Common in 1962. *Fred Ivey*

GREAT WESTERN

7037

With increasingly heavy trains Churchward's Moguls were beginning to struggle and Collett embarked on a design for a mixed traffic 4-6-0. He started by modifying Saint class locomotive No 2925 *Saint David*, which included reducing the size of the driving wheels from 6ft 8½in to 6ft and fitting a modern cab. This prototype was completed in December 1924 and after extensive trials and further modifications construction of the Hall class commenced, with No 4901 emerging in December 1928 and *Saint David* being re-numbered 4900 in the same month. Like the Castles, the Halls turned out to be a highly successful class and 257 new ones were produced up till 1943. Hawksworth, who took over as Chief Mechanical Engineer on Collett's retirement then made some changes to the design, mainly involving frames, cylinders and superheating, which culminated in the production of 71 Modified Halls between March 1944 and November 1950 (an example appears on page 100).

Above In early days, Halls ran with 3,500 gallon tenders, as illustrated here by No 4944 *Middleton Hall* on a stopping service despite the roofboards carried by the coaches. *Author's collection*

left No 4917 *Crosswood Hall* enters Birmingham Snow Hill with a southbound freight. *Great Western Trust*

Above In BR(W) days Hall class locomotives were painted in mixed traffic lined black livery until lined green livery was re-introduced in late 1956 for all passenger classes. In this photograph taken at Swindon running shed on 25 April 1954, No 5980 *Dingley Hall* (the locomotive) carries the black lined livery but is attached to a green GWR-liveried tender. *John McCann/Online Transport Archive*

Right Another locomotive design from 1924 was the 5600 class of 0-6-2 tanks, 200 of which were built between 1924 and 1928, with the final 50 being constructed by Armstrong Whitworth to relieve pressure on Swindon Works. More of the class might have been built had it not been for the fact that the new Collett generation of pannier tanks were found to be more versatile and practical, as well as being almost as powerful. The 5600 class was designed specifically for the Welsh Valley lines as replacements for the variety of 0-6-2 tanks owned by the Welsh companies absorbed by the GWR in 1922. However, some of these Welsh tanks were retained and worked alongside the Collett locomotives into the 1950s, a few even being "Greatwesternised" with GWR standard parts. It is arguable that the 5600 class was not an entirely new design because it was heavily based on the Rhymney Railway Class M and R tanks and the handful which was fitted with GWR boilers in later life very closely resembled the 5600 class. Although the Collett 0-6-2s were designed primarily for hauling heavy coal trains over short distances they also worked most of the local passenger services, entitling them to receive lined green passenger livery from the late 1950s. This is illustrated in the adjacent photograph showing No 6661 standing in appropriate surroundings against a backdrop of wagons at Pontypool Road on 7 May 1960, after arriving with the 7.40am train from Neath. *Charles Firminger*

Now for possibly Collett's most famous class, even though some might argue that it was no more than an enlarged Churchward Star. The highest nominal tractive effort for a passenger locomotive in Great Britain, 31,625lbs, had been achieved by the Castle class in 1923 but the Southern Railway's Lord Nelson class of 1926 reached 33,500 lb even though, to many, it was an inferior machine. For publicity purposes the GWR wished to regain the honour but the Company also wanted a larger locomotive type capable of taking the heaviest passenger trains over the West Country and Birmingham banks (eg Dainton and Hatton) unaided. One major obstacle was the need to strengthen some bridges on the West of England main line but Collett was told that this would be done in time for the summer 1927 timetable and that the new engine type must therefore be ready by then. Furthermore, the GWR had been invited to be the only British railway company to attend the Baltimore & Ohio Railway's centenary celebrations and transportation by ship to America would be necessary in early August. This left very little time for Collett to design a "super-Castle" but he succeeded in the task, producing a locomotive with a tractive effort of 40,300 lbs, aided by reducing the driving wheel diameter from 6ft 8½ins to 6ft 6ins, thereby recapturing the record. The class numbered thirty locomotives and the first example, No 6000 *King George V*, was unveiled on 30 June 1927. Its first public run was to haul the prestigious *Cornish Riviera Express* on 20 July 1927 non–stop from Paddington to Plymouth when it became the first locomotive to haul a ten-coach train of 338 tons tare unaided over the Devon banks. The GWR was confident that No 6000 would perform well in America and turn heads, and they were correct. The locomotive was given the honour of leading the modern locomotive cavalcade each day from 24 September to 15 October 1927 and then, on 17/18 October, No 6000 carried out a test run of 272 miles with a heavy train weighing 543 tons, taking it from Baltimore and back via Washington and Philadelphia. Under American railroad legislation, due to level crossings and unfenced track, it was required to be fitted with a bell, which it still carries to this day in preservation. The road test proved to be an outstanding success and the GWR was able to bask in its glory for several years. In all, thirty Kings were built, defeating any argument that the class was built solely for publicity purposes (ie the claim to be the most powerful engine). One engine, not 30, would have sufficed for this purpose.

Below No 6000 stands at Plymouth with a London-bound train sometime after the repositioning of the upper lamp bracket in 1933. The bell was modified following the engine's return from America by the removal of the arm on one side of the bell which was connected to the pivot and also to a cable that ran back to the cab. This was to prevent footplate crew in Britain from ringing the bell which made a sound like a fire engine! *DWK Jones collection/Online Transport Archive*

Above At the start of the GWR's centenary year in 1935, the Board told Collett they wanted streamlining to demonstrate the Company's "modern" thinking, presumably influenced by contemporary German and American practice aimed at high speed running. The fact that Gresley was in the process of producing streamlined locomotives (his A4 class) may also have prompted this decision. Collett reluctantly obliged, allegedly creating a design by attaching plasticine to a paperweight of a King. So it was that No 6014 *King Henry VII* emerged from Swindon in March 1935, six months before Gresley's *Silver Link*, but its appearance was anything but representative of Great Western Style. This so-called streamlining made no difference to the performance of No 6014 (or the similarly mistreated Castle, No 5005) and a removal process was carried out from autumn 1935 up to 1943, apart from the wedge-shaped cab which was retained on No 6014. This view of the engine at Old Oak Common depot dates from mid-1935. *G Barlow/Transport Treasury*

Below King class 4-6-0 No 6019 *King Henry V* heads out of Torquay, near Scotts Bridge, on its way to Paddington on 1 April 1962. *Les Folkard/Online Transport Archive*

Although the GWR had hundreds of very useful 0-6-0 tanks, most were elderly and were pannier tanks converted from saddletanks. Under Churchward, only five 0-6-0 tanks were built (the 1361 class dock shunters) so a priority for Collett was to design more modern versions built as pannier tanks, the large majority forming the 5700 class. As many as 863 engines of this type were built, making it Britain's second largest class in terms of numbers built for the GWR and BR, even surpassing Stanier's "Black Fives" which amounted to a mere 842! The 5700 class was constructed between 1929 and 1950, by which time Collett's successor, Hawksworth, had designed his own types of pannier tank. There were also some Collett pannier tanks such as the push and pull variants which were separately classified. All these other pannier tanks are excluded from the 863 figure. Visually, all 5700 class pannier tanks looked similar, apart from the eleven condensing engines (see page 66), except that those built from 1933 had a larger cab as previously fitted to the 5400 class pannier tanks in 1931.

This page Exuding the GWR's unique style, No 5764 prepares to leave Arley station on the heritage Severn Valley Railway. This locomotive, built in 1929, was sold by BR to London Transport in 1960 and became L95 until withdrawal in 1971. The first carriage of the train is W80969, a Hawksworth Inspection Saloon which entered service in 1948 and was withdrawn in 1973. *John Herting/Online Transport Archive*

Right Vacuum-fitted pannier tanks were used indiscriminately on both freight and passenger trains. This view from 1961 shows No 3776 approaching Axbridge station in Somerset. Axbridge was on the former Bristol & Exeter Railway's Cheddar Valley line which was later extended to link up with the East Somerset Railway (part of which is now a heritage railway of that name). The line was a victim of the Beeching Axe and was closed on 9 September 1963. *Les Folkard/ Online Transport Archive*

Below The 6700 series were only fitted with steam brakes and, as they had no vacuum brakes, were largely confined to shunting, mainly in South Wales. The third and the last engines in this line up at Newport (Pill) shed on 19 February 1961 are earlier members of the class identifiable by their lower cabs and round windows. The structure in the background is the remarkable Newport Transporter Bridge which has Grade I Listing and is one of only eight remaining in the world. *Charles Firminger*

Above Mention was made on page 64 of the 5700 class pannier tanks fitted with condensing apparatus to reduce steam emissions. This enabled them to work over London Transport underground lines to reach the GWR's Smithfield Goods Depot, replacing older, less powerful locomotives previously used. This picture features No 9700 standing at Old Oak Common on 12 November 1961. This engine was the prototype for the 9701- 9710 series built in 1933 at Swindon. It started life as No 8700, a conventional pannier tank built by Beyer Peacock in 1931, and was renumbered in 1934. *Author's collection*

Left Collett produced other pannier tank types beside the huge 5700 class. There were the 5400, 6400 and 7400 classes, the first two of which were auto-fitted and the latter two having smaller wheels. These classes were introduced in 1931, 1932 and 1936 respectively. Also there were six dock shunter pannier tanks, the 1366 class with outside cylinders, which were an updated version of Churchward's 1361 class saddletanks. These were introduced in 1934 to replace the remaining Cornwall Mineral Railway engines. This picture depicts No 1368 which ended its days at Wadebridge in Cornwall where it was photographed marshalling china clay wagons from Wenford Bridge at Dunmere Junction on 4 May 1964. Sister engine, No 1369, is preserved on the South Devon Railway. *Roy Hobbs/Online Transport Archive*

Left Small-wheeled, non-auto-fitted pannier tank No 7431 works a Blaenau Ffestiniog-Bala service in 1959. *Great Western Trust*

In 1930 Collett produced the first of his 2251 class mixed traffic 0-6-0s that were, in effect, a modernised version of the Dean Goods which they were designed to replace. No 3205 is the sole survivor of the 2251 class and was withdrawn in May 1965. While still in BR ownership and allocated to Exmouth Junction shed, the locomotive was used on the Exmoor Ranger railtour on 27 March 1965 and this view shows it banking the train at Mortehoe on the former Southern Region Barnstaple–Ilfracombe branch. Les *Folkard/Online Transport Archive*

A total of 120 engines of the 2251 class were constructed up to 1948, making these the last 0-6-0 tender engines built in Great Britain. The number series ran from 2200-2299 and 3200-3219 but the earliest examples started from No 2251 because at the time there were still some County tanks occupying the number series 2221-2250.

This page No 2211 prepares to leave Minehead with a train to Taunton in April 1946. This locomotive was the first of a batch of twenty built in 1940 with cabs lacking side windows due to wartime considerations. The branch was closed on 4 January 1971 and re-opened in part by the heritage West Somerset Railway on 28 March 1976, which now operates over some twenty miles almost into Taunton. *Arthur Davenport/Online Transport Archive*

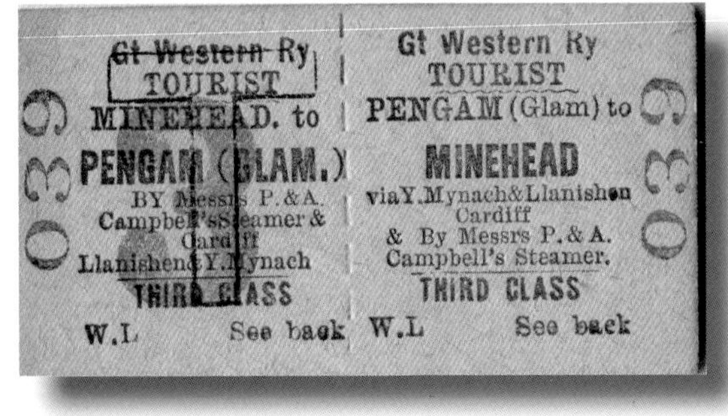

For many enthusiasts the archetypal Great Western image was a push-pull auto train powered by a lightweight, archaic-looking 1400 (4800) 0-4-2 tank. This is why four of these locomotives were acquired in working order for preservation and one became the catalyst that led to the creation of the GWS. The class originated in 1932 and was an updated version of George Armstrong's 517 class. Seventy-five were built, numbered 4800-4874, plus twenty (5800 class) not fitted for push-pull working. In 1946, the 4800 class was renumbered in the 1400 series to make way for locomotives used in the unsuccessful oil-burning experiment. The 5800 class had a shorter working life as suitable work for them dried up, with the last one being withdrawn in 1961, whereas withdrawals of the more useful 1400 class took place between 1956 and 1965. The last two, Nos 1442 and 1450, were withdrawn from Exmouth Junction depot in May 1965 and became two of the four preserved ones.

This page On a Chalford working, No 1424 leaves Gloucester Central on 8 September 1963 coupled to BR-built auto trailer W234W. *Jim Oatway*

Left No 1444 was one of the first of the class to receive BR(W) lined green passenger livery from 1956 and this view was taken at Wallingford, terminus of the short branch from Cholsey. The line has since been preserved by the heritage Cholsey & Wallingford Railway but unfortunately the original station and adjacent railway infrastructure at Wallingford no longer exists. The locomotive is attached to a Collett auto-trailer, one of 22 built between 1928 and 1933. *Author's collection*

Below 1400 class locomotives were not confined to working auto-trains although that was their principal use. On the Tiverton Junction to Hemyock branch in Devon, otherwise known as the Culm Valley Light Railway, push and pull operation was not practicable (auto trailers were too long and also there was considerable freight traffic which meant that many of the services consisted of "mixed trains"). Also, due to low speeds and tight curves a short gas-lit coach had to be used, in this case an ex-Barry Railway one. This view of No 1451 is at Uffculme. *Harry Luff/Online Transport Archive*

Above On 4 June 1937, 0-4-2 tank No 4818 and Churchward Auto-trailer No 43 wait at Malvern Link station with the 3.50pm Malvern Wells-Worcester service. *Great Western Trust*

Lower By the mid-1930s, with some trains becoming too heavy for the Mogul 2-6-0s, Collett decided to develop a medium-sized mixed traffic 4-6-0 with 5ft 8ins driving wheels – in effect a small-wheeled Hall. Eighty moguls were withdrawn and their wheels, valve motion and tenders used for this new type, the Grange class built between 1936 and 1939 and represented here by No 6836 *Estevarney Grange* at Penzance in 1958. *Alan Sainty collection*

The axle loading of the Granges meant that they were unable to take over the full range of Mogul duties and a lighter 4-6-0 type was needed. Consequently, in 1937 a further twenty Moguls were withdrawn to assist in the construction of the same number of lightweight Manor class 4-6-0s. The original intention was to rebuild all Moguls into Granges and Manors but the impending war clouds put paid to this. However, an additional ten Manors were built by BR in 1950 which were entirely "new builds". The Manors proved problematical at first with steaming difficulties but improvements were made from 1954 which brought their performance up to scratch. Yet, neither the Granges nor the Manors entirely replaced the Moguls, some of which soldiered on up to 1964, because not enough new engines had been built to replace them. Surprisingly, out of thirty Manors built, nine have been preserved and returned to running order, eight having been retrieved from Barry scrapyard and one, the GWS's No 7808 *Cookham Manor*, purchased from BR as a "runner". In contrast, none of the eighty Granges survived but the 6880 Society was formed to build a new one using as many parts as possible from "Barry hulks" and *Betton Grange* as it is called is taking shape at the Llangollen Railway.

Above No 7801 *Anthony Manor* prepares to leave Aberystwyth station in August 1962. Although the class was fairly widely distributed, they are probably most associated with the Cambrian coast route. *Jim Oatway*

The pioneering and publicity-conscious GWR started a new era in rail travel during Collett's reign when the Company purchased an unfinished diesel railcar, designed by C F Cleaver in 1933, from Hardy Railmotors Ltd, a subsidiary of the Associated Equipment Company (AEC), with streamlined bodywork by Park Royal, another AEC associated company. This heralded a fleet of railcars, with the first batch being put into service between Birmingham and Cardiff, working to fast timings. More followed, some being built by the Gloucester Railway, Carriage and Wagon Company. The entire fleet, which totalled 38, included units with buffet facilities and lavatories, as well as two parcels cars. However, the first seventeen could only be used individually as they had no buffers or drawgear and following experiments with No 18, a revised, more angular design, intended for haulage, was used for Nos 19-38. These were built at Swindon in 1940-1942 with AEC-supplied engines and transmissions. Nos 35/36 and 37/38 (No 37 later replaced by No 33) were built as "twin sets" which enabled a normal carriage to be inserted between them. In this format, these two pairs could be said to be the forerunners of the diesel multiple units that eventually replaced them, the last ones being withdrawn in 1962.

Left The streamlined diesel railcars were nicknamed "Flying Bananas", an epithet which was also applied, less appropriately perhaps, to the angular railcars. At Swindon on 20 March 1960, No 4, a 1934 vehicle with buffet awaits its preserved future as part of the National Collection. *Charles Firminger*

Above This is not one of the twin sets referred to on the page opposite but two individual railcars coupled together, Nos W27W and W30W. They are about to depart Slough for Windsor on 30 August 1958. Three railcars have been preserved, streamlined No 4 (*pictured opposite*) and two angular ones. These are No 20 on the heritage Kent & East Sussex Railway and the GWS's No 22. *Bruce Jenkins*

Below No 22 was on loan to the Severn Valley Railway, one of its previous stamping grounds in BR days, from 1967 until it was moved to Didcot in 1978. This view shows the vehicle leaving Hampton Loade for Kidderminster. *John Herting/Online Transport Archive*

Collett was responsible for several impressive carriage designs and some are shown in the images which follow. Fortunately, many are preserved on the various GWR-themed heritage railways and museums. Collett is particularly remembered for his "bow-ended" coaches, a style which he adopted up to 1933 apparently aimed at reducing the length of corridor connections for the benefit of nervous passengers when trains were running at speed. Probably the best known of his carriage designs were the eight bow-ended "Super Saloons" built in 1931-2, five of which still survive (the GWS has three and the South Devon Railway, two). In 1928, the GWR leased some Pullman carriages from the Pullman Company but decided in 1930 that it could build a better version of its own and terminated the lease in 1931. Taking full advantage of the GWR's generous loading gauge arising from the Broad Gauge era, the Super Saloons had opulent interiors which included free-standing armchairs around fixed tables. The vehicles were 9ft 7ins wide compared with the normal 9ft width, had bowed sides and recessed, angled doorways (preventing the door handles from protruding) and carried the names of members of the Royal Family on their sides. The GWR was competing with the Southern Railway for the Trans-Atlantic Ocean Liner traffic, encouraging the transport of passengers and goods to Plymouth as the first port of call rather than Southampton. The Super Saloons were used on non-stop Paddington–Plymouth Millbay trains introduced in 1931. Unfortunately, the effects of the economic recession in the early 1930s coupled with improved facilities at Southampton caused the Plymouth Trans-Atlantic traffic to dwindle and the Super Saloons were transferred to other prestigious duties such as private hire and Newbury race specials, roles which they performed until 1967.

Above The extra width and recessed angled doors of No 9118, one of two with a coupe compartment replaced by a kitchen in the mid-1930s, is clearly evident when seen against traditionally-built Special Saloon No 9002. This photograph was taken at Abingdon when I was involved in organising a GWS Open Day there in May 1970. Because of their width the Super Saloons were generally restricted to former Broad Gauge main lines and in 1935 Collett revisited this body outline in the Centenary Stock built for the *Cornish Riviera Express* (see page 76). *Author*

Below The interior of the first two vehicles, Nos 9111 and 9112, was designed and furnished by an external specialist, Trollope & Co, as shown in this illustration. Swindon Works provided the interiors of the subsequent six carriages. *Frank Dumbleton collection*

Above In the 1960s, all the Super Saloons still carried chocolate and cream livery except No 9111, formerly *King George*, and now preserved on the South Devon Railway. That coach is seen here in maroon livery at Kensington (Olympia) in June 1965 when it became part of a static International Plastics Exhibition Train (the "Interplas Express") along with another Super Saloon. *Author*

Left Restored to 1930s external condition, Super Saloons No 9112 *Queen Mary* and No 9118 *Princess Elizabeth*, forming part of the mainline GWS Vintage Train, speed through Appleford on their way from Paddington to Birmingham on 15 May 1976. The train is hauled by No 6998 *Burton Agnes Hall* piloted by No 5900 *Hinderton Hall*, the latter making its railtour debut. *Author*

As part of the celebrations for the GWR Centenary in 1935, twenty-six carriages known as "Centenary Stock" and resembling the Super Saloons in outline were produced specifically for the GWR's most prestigious train, the *Cornish Riviera Express*. Surprisingly, only one Centenary carriage survives today: Restaurant car No 9635 which can be found at Didcot.

Right The Cornish Riviera Express formed of Centenary stock and hauled by No 6017 *King Edward IV* passes beach huts at Dawlish in August 1936. *Great Western Trust*

Below As seen here, Centenary brake third No 4577, one of six such vehicles, remained in service long enough to acquire BR maroon livery. *Great Western Trust*

Above After the lifting of the steam ban following No 6000's triumphant H P Bulmer's Return to Steam specials in October 1971 (see page 124) the GWS ran its first steam railtour on 1 October 1972 using No 6998 *Burton Agnes Hall.* The train is seen at Heyford on the outward journey north. The formation included two of the Society's own coaches, both Collett designs: No 5952, an 8-compartment All-Third from 1935 and No 1289, an "Excursion" open Third with Art Deco interior (see page 78) built in 1937. *Author*

Left Photographed at Bridgnorth on the Severn Valley Railway on 19 September 1971, this is Collett No 6562, a Brake Composite (ie containing more than one class) dating from 1938. Most of the accommodation is Third Class but there are two First Class compartments at the far end. *Doris Davenport/Online Transport Archive*

Right In 1935, the first batch of Collett "Excursion" thirds entered service, with a central corridor which produced the "open" internal layout that we are all familiar with today. Although other companies had already built coaches with this configuration for excursion and party travel, the interiors were usually more basic whereas the GWR version, with its Art Deco fittings and birch panelling inlaid with mahogany, was anything but spartan. This is Didcot's carriage No 1289 dating from 1937.

Right and below right At the opposite end of the spectrum, two 12-wheeled Special Saloons, Nos 9001 and 9002, were built in 1940 and intended for railway and governmental VIP use. Indeed, they are believed to have been used by Winston Churchill and General Eisenhower during the Second World War. The interior comprised a main saloon (with radio and loose furniture), dining room, coupe compartment and kitchen. Both coaches had a refit in the early 1950s and were available for hire as mobile conference rooms, but saw little use. Both are now preserved and restored, No 9001 being based at the Buckinghamshire Railway Centre and No 9002 at Didcot. The latter was acquired by the GWS in 1967, apparently soon after HM The Queen Mother had travelled in it to Newbury Races. Following a comprehensive restoration, it was "re-launched" at Didcot by HRH The Princess Royal in 2003. These interior shots show the magnificent main saloon and the vintage kitchen equipment. *Frank Dumbleton-all*

Above and above right These photographs show two types of 1930s dining facilities. First class passengers are dining in a wide-bodied Centenary restaurant-car, with quartered oak panelling and walnut inlay trim. A different clientele is being served in one of the five 1938-built twelve-wheel buffet-cars which were of normal width and used on cross-country services. The internal layout included a buffet counter with stools as well as bench seats with tables.
Great Western Trust-both

Left In contrast, here is a goods vehicle from the Collett era. This scene at Abingdon Open Day in May 1970 features an ASMO Motor Car Van. This particular one is No 116954 built in 1930. On this day it was possible to demonstrate that three Austin Sevens could fit inside, the first two of which were mine. In the background are Special Saloon No 9002 and Super Saloon No 9118. *Author*

Aviation

The GWR was the first British railway company to set up its own airline to operate scheduled services, marketing it as Great Western Railway Air Services. Using a triple- engined Westland Wessex six-seater aircraft leased from Imperial Airways painted in GWR chocolate and cream livery and carrying the noteworthy registration G-AAGW, the first public flight took place on 12 April 1933 between Plymouth Airport, Haldon Aerodrome (for Teignmouth and Torquay) and Cardiff. On 22 May 1933, the service was extended to Birmingham Airport. However, with the onset of winter, services ceased on 1 October 1933 and never restarted under the GWR's individual name. Instead, the other three mainline railway companies joined the GWR and Imperial Airways to form a consortium called Railway Air Services (RAS) based at Croydon Airport which started commercial operations on 1 May 1934 and soon operated a wide range of domestic and cross-Channel routes. Apart from a short cessation at the start of the Second World War RAS continued operating until 1947 when its services were taken over by the newly formed State airline, British European Airways (BEA).

Alongside its RAS involvement the GWR also formed, in 1938, a joint venture with the Southern Railway called Great Western & Southern Air Lines. This operated in association with RAS and Olley Air Services (Gordon Olley piloted the GWR's inaugural flight in 1933), taking over Channel Air Ferries' routes in 1939.

Right Westland Aircraft placed this advertisement featuring G-AAGW and a GWR King-hauled train in a number of aeronautical magazines in May 1933. *Aviationancestry.co.uk*

Far right This RAS luggage label was issued to my parents who were in Reserved Occupations during the Second World War and travelled by RAS between Liverpool and Dublin. *Author*

Below This futuristic, imaginatively designed timetable cover dates from 22 May 1933, reflecting the start of GWR Air Services to Birmingham. It also heralds a very early use of the roundel motif. *Björn Larsson/Airline Timetable Images*

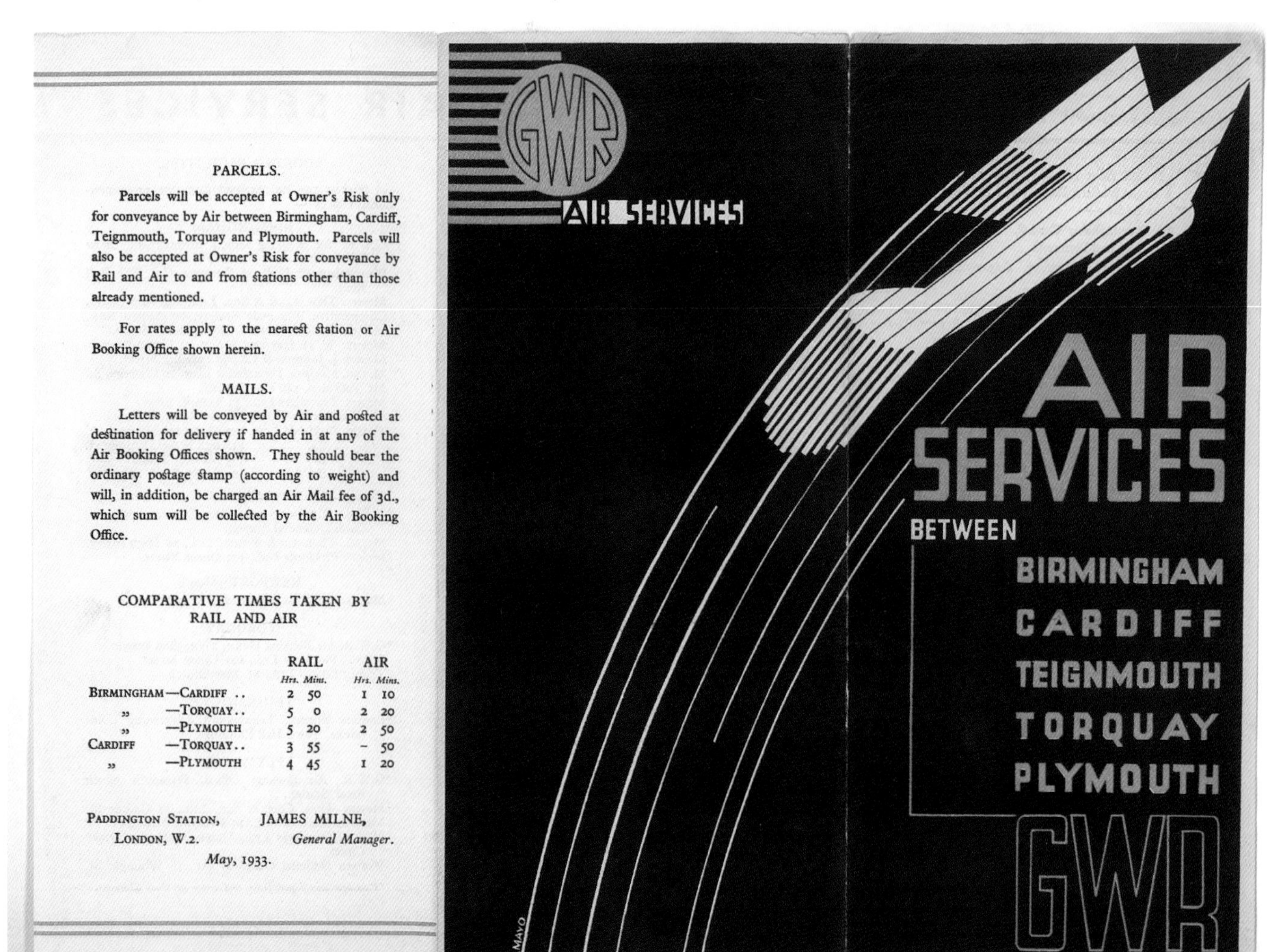

PARCELS.

Parcels will be accepted at Owner's Risk only for conveyance by Air between Birmingham, Cardiff, Teignmouth, Torquay and Plymouth. Parcels will also be accepted at Owner's Risk for conveyance by Rail and Air to and from stations other than those already mentioned.

For rates apply to the nearest station or Air Booking Office shown herein.

MAILS.

Letters will be conveyed by Air and posted at destination for delivery if handed in at any of the Air Booking Offices shown. They should bear the ordinary postage stamp (according to weight) and will, in addition, be charged an Air Mail fee of 3d., which sum will be collected by the Air Booking Office.

COMPARATIVE TIMES TAKEN BY RAIL AND AIR

		RAIL		AIR	
		Hrs.	Mins.	Hrs.	Mins.
BIRMINGHAM	—CARDIFF ..	2	50	1	10
"	—TORQUAY ..	5	0	2	20
"	—PLYMOUTH	5	20	2	50
CARDIFF	—TORQUAY ..	3	55	-	50
"	—PLYMOUTH	4	45	1	20

PADDINGTON STATION, LONDON, W.2.

JAMES MILNE, *General Manager*.

May, 1933.

RAS De Havilland Express DH 86, G-AEFH *Neptune*, stands at Croydon Airport in 1938 in front of the air traffic control tower and terminal building since preserved which look exactly the same today even though the airport closed in 1959. One former RAS aircraft has been preserved in RAS livery, DH 89A Dragon Rapide, G-ALXT *Star of Scotia* dating from 1944. It is owned by the Science Museum and currently stored at Wroughton. An older ex-RAS machine, DH84 Dragon, G-ADDI *City of Cardiff*, later named *Island Maid*, built in 1935 and subsequently owned by Chrisair is still flying today in America. I travelled in it in 1964, which was my first flight in an aeroplane. You can take a flight in it on YouTube, filmed in 2013! *Malcolm Knight collection/Online Transport Archive*

The Hawksworth Era

When Charles Collett retired in 1941 he was succeeded as CME by Frederick Hawksworth who stayed in post until 1949. Hawksworth took over at a difficult time: Britain was embroiled in the Second World War with locomotive building restrictions coming into force, materials being in short supply and Great Western innovation having stagnated, mainly due to Collett clinging on to his position until he was almost 70 years old. Hawksworth was no youngster either, filling the role aged 57. He had joined the GWR in 1898 and progressed through the Drawing Office. He then became Principal Assistant to Collett in 1932 when William Stanier was headhunted by the LMS. As CME, Hawksworth created some memorable designs: the Modified Halls (covered in the Collett chapter), County 4-6-0s, three types of distinctive pannier tanks, flat-sided welded tenders for 4-6-0s and modern coaches with sloping roof ends. He also increased superheating to improve locomotive performance. It has to be said however that, apart from the Modified Halls, the other types which he designed were arguably not needed, as well as falling outside previous standardisation policy. They also had short working lives although this was not because they were sub-standard. Hawksworth was not to know how quickly dieselisation would take hold. Hawksworth retired at the end of 1949 under BR(W) auspices.

The County 4-6-0s certainly looked different from previous GWR 2-cylinder 4-6-0s. They had an unusual driving wheel size (6ft 3ins) and very high boiler pressure (subsequently reduced partly due to rough riding) but, most noticeably, the engines carried horizontal nameplates (an idea seemingly copied from the two Collett streamliners) and flat-sided tenders. No 1000 *County of Middlesex* was the first of the 30-strong class and was built in August 1945. This is No 1025 *County of Radnor* backing out of Paddington station on 23 October 1948. *Neil Davenport/Online Transport Archive*

Left Apart from No 1000, the Counties were built with single chimneys but subsequent fitting of double chimneys improved their previous indifferent performance, though not their appearance. Thirty 4000 gallon flat-sided tenders were built for the County class. These were 8ft 6ins wide to match the wide cabs fitted to this class and could carry 7 tons of coal. 107 further Hawksworth tenders were built and fitted to some other 4-6-0s, eg Castles and Halls, but these were only 8ft wide and limited to 6 tons of coal. This picture depicts No 1015 *County of Gloucester* at Old Oak Common on 15 March 1959. *Alan Sainty collection*

Below Loco spotters at Cardiff (General) look on as No 1023 *County of Oxford* passes through with a milk and parcels train on 5 April 1962. The class was withdrawn between September 1962 and November 1964 and none was preserved. This omission is being rectified by the GWS which is building a replacement No 1014 *County of Glamorgan*, the locomotive being chosen in recognition of the location of Barry scrapyard and the fact that the County Council supplied the frames and boiler for the new build from Barry hulks. *Ian Dunnett/Online Transport Archive*

Hawksworth's 9400 class pannier tanks numbered 210, the first ten of which, Nos 9400-9409, were constructed in 1947, making these the last locomotives built by the GWR before Nationalisation. The remaining class members were all built by outside contractors through to October 1956 when No 3409 emerged for a service life of barely eight years. This was by no means the worst case. No 8447 managed less than five years (October 1954 – May 1959). The engines were very powerful for their size, possessing the same boilers and cylinders as the 2251 class 0-6-0 tender engines, although this created the disadvantage of restricting their route availability compared with traditional pannier tanks.

Above Among their heavyweight duties were empty stock workings at Paddington, demonstrated here by No 9422. *Alan Sainty collection*

Left Four pannier tanks stand at Old Oak Common against the backdrop of the distinctive coaling stage/water tower structure on 13 October 1963. The first in line is No 8420. *Alan Sainty collection*

The next pannier tank type designed by Hawksworth was the 1500 class of ten locomotives, with No 1500 making its debut in June 1949. These engines were completely non-standard, having outside cylinders, Walschaerts valve gear and no running plate. With their heavy weight and short wheelbase they were also severely route restricted and were generally limited to empty stock workings and heavy shunting duties. The first six were based at Old Oak Common and the remaining four in Wales such as No 1509 (*right*), photographed at Newport High Street on 2 August 1958. This engine, along with Nos 1501 and 1502, ended up with the National Coal Board and the Severn Valley Railway has restored No 1501 using parts from the other two which have since been scrapped. *Alan Sainty collection*

Below In contrast with his other 0-6-0 tanks, Hawksworth's final pannier tank design was his lightweight 1600 class with 4ft 1½in driving wheels, totalling seventy machines and were designed to replace Dean's 2021 class. The 1600 class entered service between October 1949 and May 1955 and were withdrawn between 1959 and 1966, with some barely working for five years. This view at Swindon depicts No 1658 working an unadvertised workmen's train to Highworth, on a former light railway which closed to passengers in 1953. The last of these special trains for workers employed at Swindon Works ran on 3 August 1962. *Alan Sainty collection*

A dramatically different locomotive from the Hawksworth era was gas turbine-electric locomotive No 18000. It was ordered by the GWR in 1946 partly because of concerns about supplies of good quality coal which the Company's engines relied upon for good performance. The order, placed on Brown, Boveri of Switzerland, coincided with the conversion of some steam locomotives to oil burning (see page 41). However, No 18000 did not arrive at Swindon until February 1950 and since this was after Nationalisation it always carried BR livery. It was initially painted black with a silver stripe along the waistline and silver numerals (no brass or cast iron numberplates!) but gained locomotive Brunswick green in 1957, as portrayed in the picture (above) taken at Swindon Works on 20 March 1960. The locomotive was fitted with an auxiliary diesel engine for start-up purposes and was meant to be fuel efficient, but this was not the case unless it was running at top speed. No 18000 was powerful because the GWR wanted to avoid the situation where the LMS had ordered a large mainline diesel locomotive which turned out to be underpowered and incapable of hauling express trains unless it was paired with its twin. Nevertheless, the power output of No 18000 was no greater than a King and was limited to 90mph whereas Kings, once they were fitted with double chimneys, regularly exceeded this limit. No 18000 had a troublesome history and was often out of service due to defects. It was withdrawn in December 1960 and returned to Switzerland where it was used for research. Stripped of its inner workings, the locomotive was repatriated in the 1990s and is on display at Didcot. A British-built gas turbine locomotive was also ordered by the GWR (No 18100), entering service in 1951. It ran on aviation fuel (kerosene) and was even more expensive to run than 18000 which used heavy fuel oil. No 18100 was withdrawn in January 1958 and converted into an electric locomotive. *Charles Firminger*

We end the Hawksworth chapter with external shots of two carriages.

Above Displaying its characteristic sloping roof ends, this is W922W, an all-third from 1948 and one of seventy such vehicles built under Diagram C82. *Great Western Trust*

Below Ordered by BR in 1951 and built up to 1954, the post-war auto trailers Nos 220-244 were the first new ones to emerge since the 1930s. Seen at Wrexham Central on an Ellesmere train on 21 July 1962 hauled by 0-4-2 tank No 1458, W231W, complete with curtains, is now preserved at Didcot in its original BR crimson lake and cream ("blood & custard") livery as seen on W922W above. *Charles Firminger*

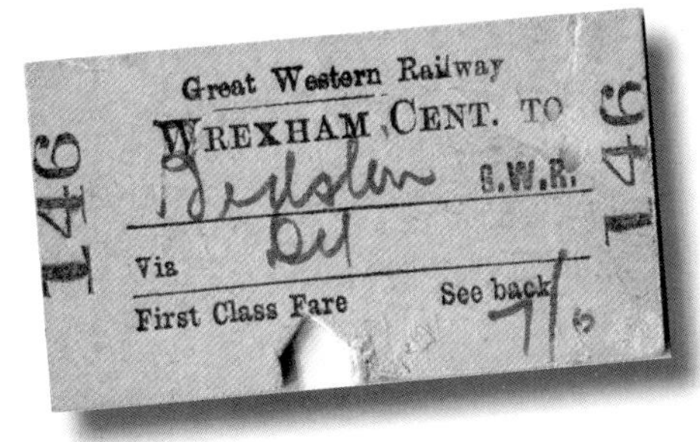

Publicity

The GWR appreciated the value of advertising from the outset but did not set up a specific department until 1886, and that was within another part of management. However, it was the early 1900s which saw a greater effort made, with the GWR's first book being published in 1904 on the *Cornish Riviera Express*, coinciding with the introduction of the train from London to Penzance, the title of which was chosen by readers of the Railway Magazine in a competition. There was much to publicise: a non-stop journey to Plymouth of some 245 miles through impressive scenery starting in the Thames Valley through the Vale of the White Horse and eventually alongside the Devon sea wall and over Brunel's wonderful Royal Albert bridge into Cornwall. This book was followed in 1906 by the famous publication, Holiday Haunts, which introduced the slogan The Holiday Line. In 1924 the advertising department became a stand-alone publicity department, promoting the Railway not only to adults but also to the younger generation through items such as jigsaws and engine "spotting books"(although the first of the latter appeared as early as 1911). Some of these and other items, from the Author's collection and photographed by Frank Dumbleton, as well as items held by the Great Western Trust are reproduced below and on the eight pages which follow:

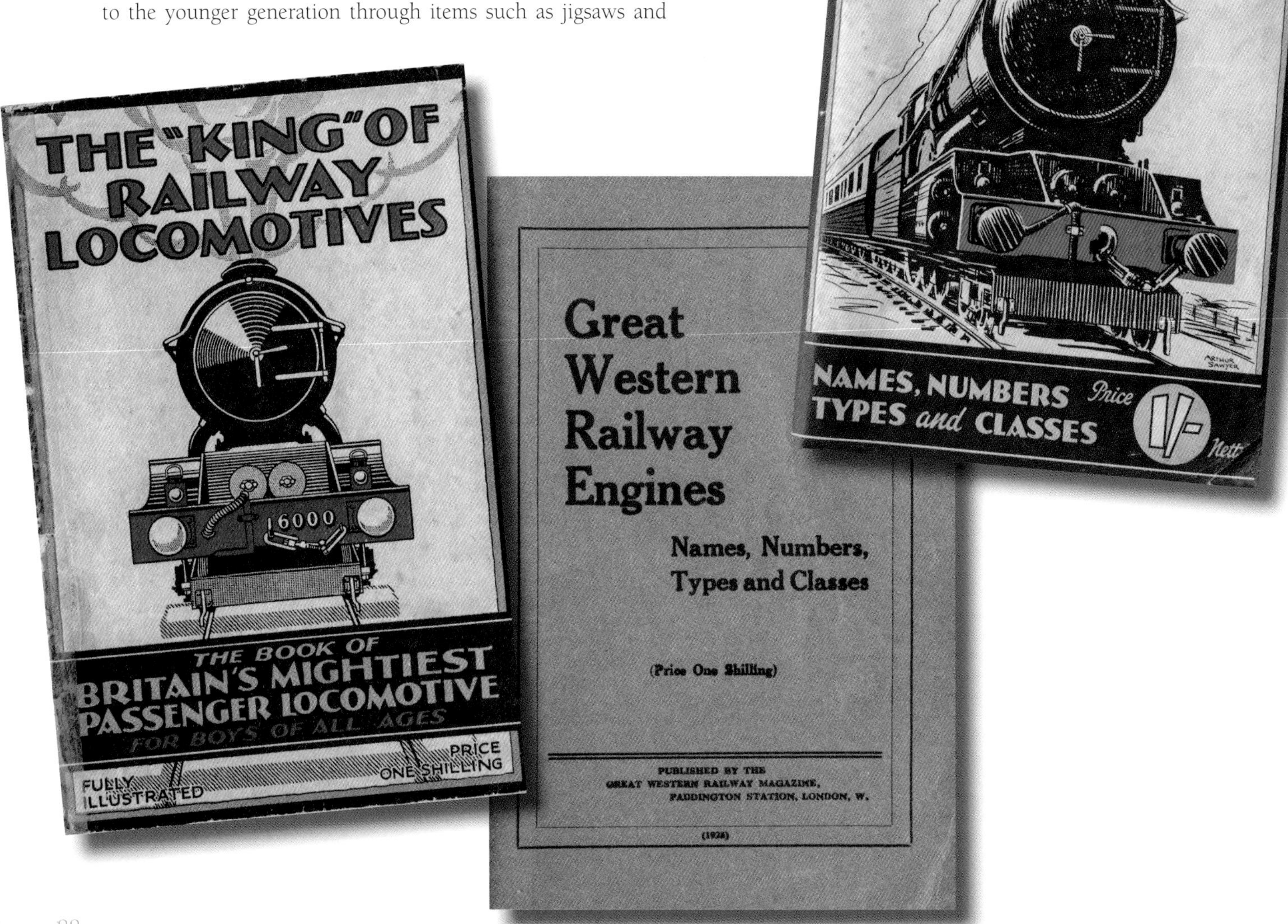

JIG-SAW PUZZLE
DOMINE DIRIGE NOS
ABOUT
150
PIECES
ABOUT
150
PIECES

Opposite page This was a breakfast menu available on a Paddington-Swansea train on 19 December 1932. On the reverse of the menu is a map of the GWR system which identifies GWR hotels including the one illustrated on the front.

MANOR HOUSE HOTEL. MORETONHAMPSTEAD DEVON.

MENU

Swansea
Car (4)

December 19th, 1932

TABLE D'HÔTE BREAKFAST 3/6

Corn Flakes and Cream
Porridge and Cream
Finnon Haddock
Grilled Kippers
Bacon and Eggs
Ham and Tomatoes
Sausage and Sauté Potatoes
Kidney and Bacon
Omelette (to order)
Cold Meats
Jam, Marmalade and Honey
Tea or Coffee

SHORT BREAKFAST 2/6

Porridge or Boiled Eggs or Cold Ham
Tea or Coffee
Rolls, Butter and Preserves.

Grape Fruit, per portion, 6d. extra.

GREAT WESTERN RAILWAY.

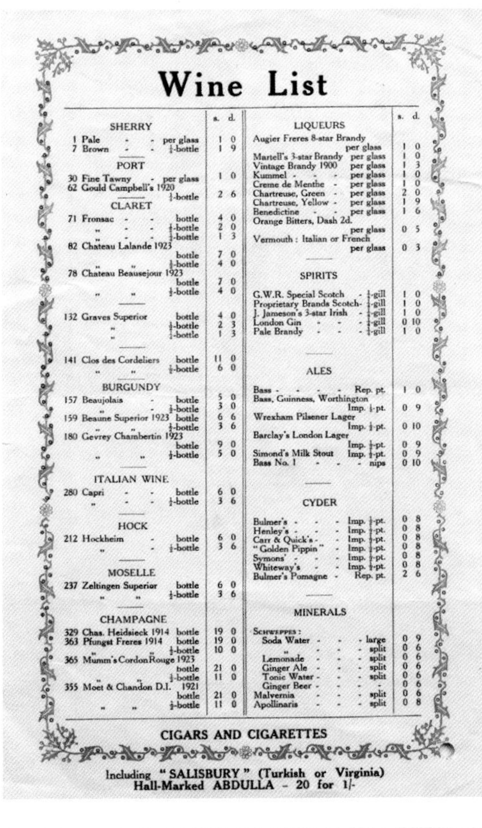

Wine List

		s.	d.
SHERRY			
1 Pale	per glass	1	0
7 Brown	½-bottle	1	9
PORT			
30 Fine Tawny	per glass	1	0
62 Gould Campbell's 1920	½-bottle	2	6
CLARET			
71 Fronsac	bottle	4	0
"	½-bottle	2	0
"	¼-bottle	1	3
82 Chateau Lalande 1923	bottle	7	0
" "	½-bottle	4	0
78 Chateau Beausejour 1923	bottle	7	0
" "	½-bottle	4	0
132 Graves Superior	bottle	4	0
"	½-bottle	2	3
"	¼-bottle	1	3
141 Clos des Cordeliers	bottle	11	0
" "	½-bottle	6	0
BURGUNDY			
157 Beaujolais	bottle	5	0
"	½-bottle	3	0
159 Beaune Superior 1923	bottle	6	6
" "	½-bottle	3	6
180 Gevrey Chambertin 1923	bottle	9	0
" "	½-bottle	5	0
ITALIAN WINE			
280 Capri	bottle	6	0
"	½-bottle	3	6
HOCK			
212 Hockheim	bottle	6	0
"	½-bottle	3	6
MOSELLE			
237 Zeltingen Superior	bottle	6	0
" "	½-bottle	3	6
CHAMPAGNE			
329 Chas. Heidsieck 1914	bottle	19	0
363 Pfungst Freres 1914	bottle	19	0
" "	½-bottle	10	0
365 Mumm's Cordon Rouge 1923	bottle	21	0
" "	½-bottle	11	0
355 Moet & Chandon D.I. 1921	bottle	21	0
" "	½-bottle	11	0

		s.	d.
LIQUEURS			
Augier Freres 8-star Brandy	per glass	1	0
Martell's 3-star Brandy	per glass	1	0
Vintage Brandy 1900	per glass	1	3
Kummel	per glass	1	0
Creme de Menthe	per glass	1	0
Chartreuse, Green	per glass	2	0
Chartreuse, Yellow	per glass	1	9
Benedictine	per glass	1	6
Orange Bitters, Dash 2d.	per glass	0	5
Vermouth : Italian or French	per glass	0	3
SPIRITS			
G.W.R. Special Scotch	⅙-gill	1	0
Proprietary Brands Scotch	⅙-gill	1	0
J. Jameson's 3-star Irish	⅙-gill	1	0
London Gin	⅙-gill	0	10
Pale Brandy	⅙-gill	1	0
ALES			
Bass	Rep. pt.	1	0
Bass, Guinness, Worthington	Imp. ½-pt.	0	9
Wrexham Pilsener Lager	Imp. ½-pt.	0	10
Barclay's London Lager	Imp. ½-pt.	0	9
Simond's Milk Stout	Imp. ½-pt.	0	9
Bass No. 1	nips	0	10
CYDER			
Bulmer's	Imp. ½-pt.	0	8
Henley's	Imp. ½-pt.	0	8
Carr & Quick's	Imp. ½-pt.	0	8
"Golden Pippin"	Imp. ½-pt.	0	8
Symons'	Imp. ½-pt.	0	8
Whiteway's	Imp. ½-pt.	0	8
Bulmer's Pomagne	Rep. pt.	2	6
MINERALS			
SCHWEPPES:			
Soda Water	large	0	9
"	split	0	6
Lemonade	split	0	6
Ginger Ale	split	0	6
Tonic Water	split	0	6
Ginger Beer	-	0	6
Malvernia	split	0	6
Apollinaris	split	0	8

CIGARS AND CIGARETTES

Including "SALISBURY" (Turkish or Virginia)
Hall-Marked ABDULLA – 20 for 1/-

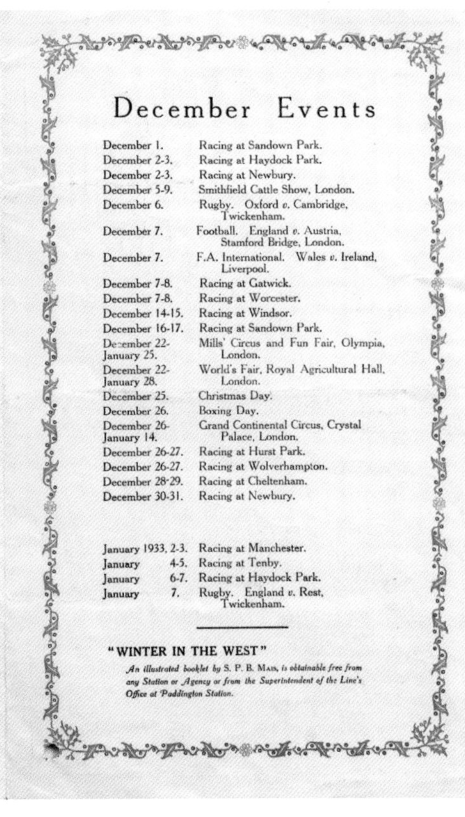

December Events

December 1.	Racing at Sandown Park.
December 2-3.	Racing at Haydock Park.
December 2-3.	Racing at Newbury.
December 5-9.	Smithfield Cattle Show, London.
December 6.	Rugby. Oxford *v.* Cambridge, Twickenham.
December 7.	Football. England *v.* Austria, Stamford Bridge, London.
December 7.	F.A. International. Wales *v.* Ireland, Liverpool.
December 7-8.	Racing at Gatwick.
December 7-8.	Racing at Worcester.
December 14-15.	Racing at Windsor.
December 16-17.	Racing at Sandown Park.
December 22- January 25.	Mills' Circus and Fun Fair, Olympia, London.
December 22- January 28.	World's Fair, Royal Agricultural Hall, London.
December 25.	Christmas Day.
December 26.	Boxing Day.
December 26- January 14.	Grand Continental Circus, Crystal Palace, London.
December 26-27.	Racing at Hurst Park.
December 26-27.	Racing at Wolverhampton.
December 28-29.	Racing at Cheltenham.
December 30-31.	Racing at Newbury.
January 1933, 2-3.	Racing at Manchester.
January 4-5.	Racing at Tenby.
January 6-7.	Racing at Haydock Park.
January 7.	Rugby. England *v.* Rest, Twickenham.

"WINTER IN THE WEST"

An illustrated booklet by S. P. B. Mais, is obtainable free from any Station or Agency or from the Superintendent of the Line's Office at Paddington Station.

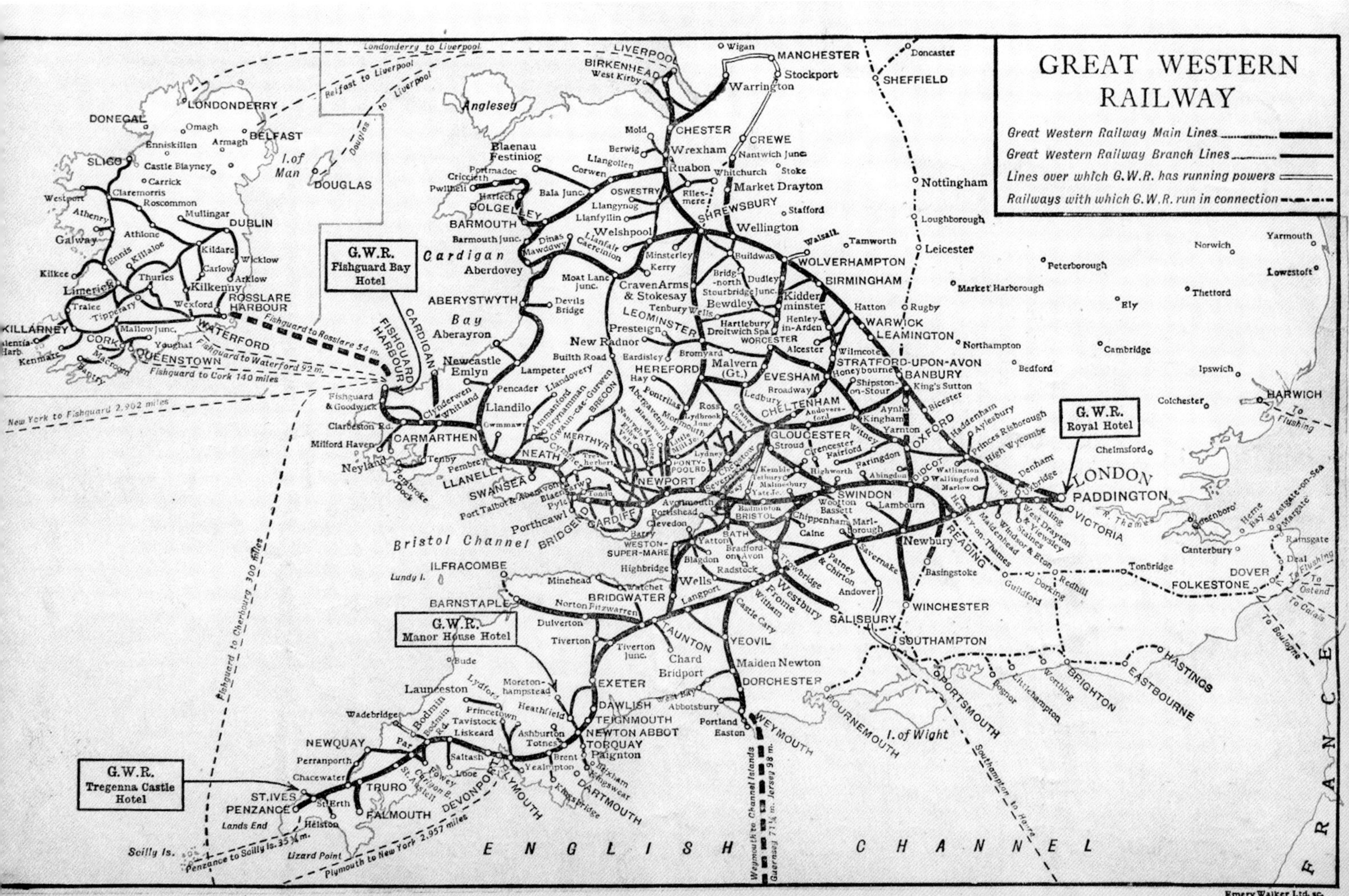

OXFORD
LONDON
Great Western Railway
WINDSOR RACES
CORNWALL

TRAVEL BY G.W.R.
NEWQUAY
IN THE CORNISH RIVIERA
SAFE SURF BATHING
SOMERSET
GREAT WESTERN RAILWAY
WALES
TOURIST AND EXCURSION TICKETS
GREAT WESTERN RAILWAY
WATERFORD.
UNSURPASSED FOR HAPPY HOLIDAYS
GLORIOUS SCENERY & IRISH SPORTS
GREAT WESTERN RAILWAY C°
MANOR HOUSE HOTEL
FISHING RIGHTS ONLY
NOTICE
LADIES' ROOM
3RD CLASS
WAITING ROOM
3RD CLASS

As well as items such as books, handbills, games, menus and silverware used in GWR hotels and restaurant cars etc there were of course the iconic posters normally affixed to station walls. To add to the historic ambience of Didcot Railway Centre the tiled access tunnel to the depot, dating from steam days, has been retained, in stark contrast with the modernised passageway from the station concourse leading to the platforms, and several examples of these posters have been mounted to give visitors a flavour of the GWR era (*opposite*). There is also a museum on site containing many GWR artefacts including, as seen opposite upper, posters, cast iron notices and catering items, the latter carrying the GWR coat of arms, monogram or 1930s roundel motif.

Right This GWR platform ticket machine, wooden bench (with dozing waxwork!) and joint GWR/Southern Railway poster are on display at Steam Museum, Swindon. *Frank Dumbleton-all*

Far left Holiday Guide cover (1931)

Left Winter Resorts Guide cover (September 1923)

Right Autumn Holiday Tickets timetable cover (1931)

Far right Christmas Holiday Tickets timetable cover (1931)
Great Western Trust-all

Following the disembarkation at Plymouth of some passengers travelling from America to London who preferred to finish their journey by fast train, the GWR found this novel way of filling up ocean liners for the remainder of the journey to London: travel by train from London to Plymouth and return by luxury ship! *Great Western Trust*

ENJOY A WEEK-END CIRCULAR TOUR by G.W.R and OCEAN LINER

Passengers joining Cunard Liners at Plymouth for London have full use of the public accommodation on the Ships, including Dining, Drawing, Dancing Rooms, Gymnasia, etc. Private Cabins are also provided.

The fares quoted in this folder cover all necessary meals on the Ships.

All information regarding train services from London to Plymouth in connection with these Cruises will be gladly furnished by the Supt. of the Line, G.W.R., Paddington Station, London, W.2.

Full particulars as to Sailings, etc., can be obtained on application to :—

LONDON : Cunard S.S. Co.,
26/27 Cockspur St., S.W.1.
51 Bishopsgate, E.C.

PLYMOUTH : Cunard S.S. Co.,
2 Millbay Rd.

WEEK-END SEA CRUISES BY CUNARD LINERS FROM PLYMOUTH TO LONDON

CUNARD OCEAN LINERS calling at Plymouth (usually on Saturdays) afford an opportunity of at least 25 or 26 hours' sea travel from Plymouth to London, passing close to the Channel Islands and Cherbourg, calling at Havre, and subsequently proceeding within sight of the South Coast of England and passing up the Estuary of the Thames.

Passengers taking these trips have the enjoyment of trans-oceanic travel luxury.

ROUND TRIP FARE

LONDON-PLYMOUTH-LONDON
(Paddington Station)

(including Plymouth Dock Charges, Rail and Liner [Cabin] Fares.)

First Class on Rail—
£4 19s. 0d.

Third Class on Rail—
£4 5s. 0d.

BY CUNARD OCEAN LINER
PLYMOUTH TO LONDON

TRAVEL BY GREAT WESTERN RAILWAY from LONDON to PLYMOUTH and ENJOY the PLEASURE of an OCEAN LINER trip from PLYMOUTH to LONDON.

BY G.W.R. RESTAURANT CAR EXPRESS
LONDON TO PLYMOUTH

In the earlier years of the 20th century the GWR had concentrated on publicity aimed at attracting passenger traffic, eg Winter Resorts promoting the West Country's warmer climate and consequent medical benefits, excellent hotels, lovely scenery, etc. This continued throughout the 1930s with the promotion of the "Holiday Line" and such attractions as Spas. The brochure on Spas would cover such places as Bath, Cheltenham, Malvern, Builth Wells and Llanrindod Wells. However, it was not until the Railway Grouping of 1922/3 that the GWR put greater effort into promoting freight traffic. An example of this was the Docks booklet, the absorption of Welsh railway companies into the GWR having greatly increased the Company's ownership of Docks. Existing GWR docks such as Millbay, Falmouth, Fishguard, Avonmouth and Brentford were now joined by others including Cardiff, Alexandra (Newport), Burry Port and Port Talbot.

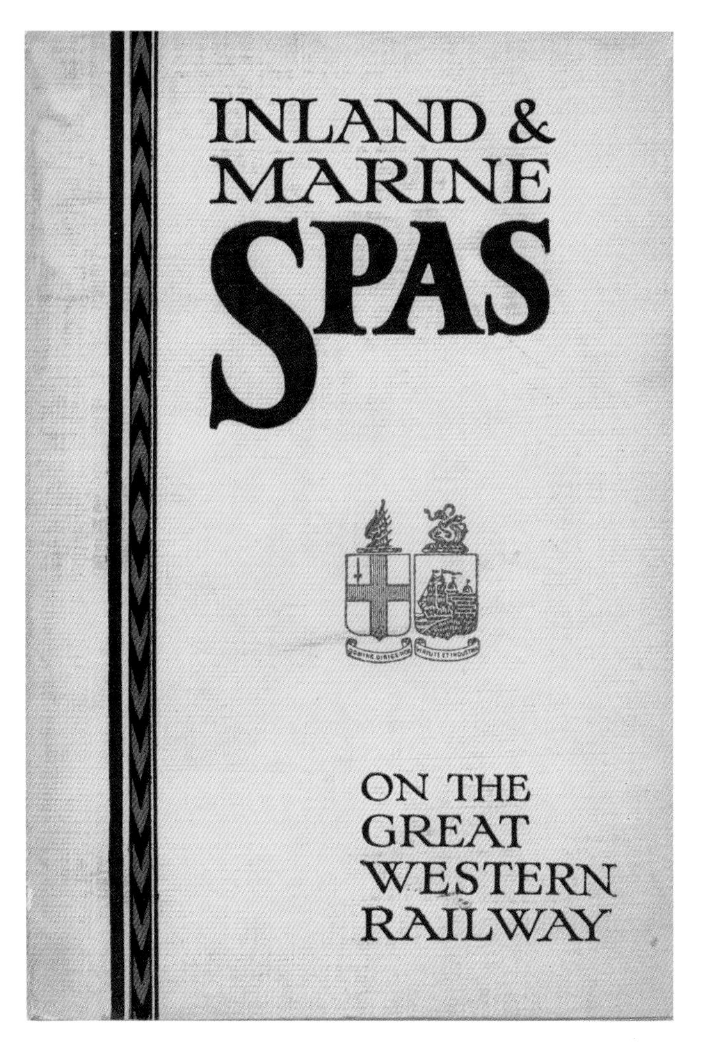

Left Inland & Marine Spas Guide cover (1924). *Great Western Trust*

Right Docks of the GWR Booklet cover (July 1931). *Great Western Trust*

Through its posters and leaflets/brochures the GWR exploited the attractiveness of the West Country as a holiday destination to reach by using its trains(and to deter passengers from travelling by the rival Southern Railway!), characterising itself as the "Holiday Line". Many of the resorts were reached by GWR branch lines such as those to Brixham, Newquay, Looe and St Ives but the delights of travelling along the coastal section between Exeter and Newton Abbott were also extolled. These two photographs taken at Dawlish in Devon illustrate the scenes captured in publicity material. A King class locomotive hauls a Cornwall-bound express in the 1930s and Castle class locomotive No 5071 *Spitfire*, the first of a batch named after Second World War aircraft, emerges from Parsons Tunnel, hewn through the sandstone rock. *Great Western Trust; Les Folkard/Online Transport Archive*

Apart from producing posters of exotic-looking places to visit on the GWR network its publicity machine was keen to publicise the power and speed of its engines and the attraction of travelling on its named trains. On power, there were books on the Kings and excursions to Swindon to visit their birthplace. On speed there were record breaking runs such as *City of Truro*'s so-called record of 102.3mph, although it is now doubtful whether that maximum was reached but at least the claim ensured that the engine was preserved (albeit by the LNER!). Ironically, this fast run on 9 May 1904 between Exeter and Taunton of a trans-Atlantic mail train was initially hushed up by the GWR because of accidents involving speed which occurred on other railways and was not publicised until 1922. The *Cheltenham Flyer*, the name given to the *Cheltenham Spa Express*, was claimed by the GWR to be the world's fastest regular service from 1931-1935 (albeit only on the level Swindon-Paddington leg of the journey) with an average speed of 71.4mph over the 77.3 mile distance. The record was claimed on 14 September 1931 when No 5000 *Launceston Castle*, driven by JW Street, completed the journey in 59.36 minutes. Subsequently, No 5006 *Treganna Castle* achieved an average speed of 81.6mph on 6 June 1932 for this train, again a world record. The GWR ensured that the train engine always carried a headboard proclaiming its record. This was a rare exception to the GWR's policy of not placing train names on their engines, generally confining names to carriage roofboards. Most named trains that readers will be familiar with were introduced by BR(W) in the 1950s with engine headboards but a few named trains dated back to GWR days, eg the *Cornish Riviera Express* (1904), the *Torbay Express* (1923), the *Cambrian Coast Express* (1927) and the *Bristolian* (1935).

This page No 3440 *City of Truro* stands at Newton Abbot in 1960 during a station lighting replacement programme. *Les Folkard/Online Transport Archive*

Right The Cheltenham Flyer heads towards London through Slough behind rebuilt pacific, now Castle class 4-6-0 No 111 *Viscount Churchill. Railway Wonders of the World*

Below The west of Shrewsbury stage of the Cambrian Coast Express stops at Dovey Junction behind Manor class 4-6-0 No 7823 *Hook Norton Manor* in August 1962. *Jim Oatway*

Joint Working

In order to pursue its own interests the GWR operated a number of joint lines with other railway companies. The best known, at least to Londoners, was probably the joint line with the Great Central Railway (the LNER from 1923) from Northolt Junction, West London, to Ashendon Junction, Buckinghamshire. This enabled the Great Central to reach London (Marylebone) more conveniently than having to use the Metropolitan Railway's busy tracks and allowed the GWR to introduce 2-hour trains to Birmingham from 1910, in direct competition with the LNWR, by no longer having to go via Didcot and Oxford, saving nearly twenty route miles. Other joint lines, in partnership with the LNWR (LMS from 1923), enabled the GWR to reach Birkenhead and Manchester.

Left Working over the GW/GC Joint Line sometime before 1914 (because the engine still carries the brass beading on the splashers) Saint class locomotive No 2977 *Robertson* hauls a down Birmingham train over Ruislip water troughs. The train is composed of stock belonging to one of the Southern Railway predecessor companies. *Great Western Trust*

Below On 3 May 1962, Hawksworth Modified Hall No 7902 *Eaton Mascot Hall* is seen near Beaconsfield with an up freight. *Alan Sainty collection*

Above There is no Great Western Style applied to this station building which is Manchester Exchange, closed in 1969. The GWR reached there, until it discontinued its services in 1943, by using its own line to Chester, then taking the GWR/LNWR joint route to Warrington Bank Quay and finally by utilising its running rights over the LNWR's tracks via Eccles. This photograph depicts No 6816 *Frankton Grange* about to leave Manchester Exchange for Chester, hopefully after the railwayman has stopped leaning on the buffer! *Author's collection*

Below Birkenhead depot was a joint GWR/LNWR enterprise and the GWR had a fleet of ancient Armstrong former class 850/1901 saddletanks converted to pannier tanks, for use in its docks (note boiler mounted warning bell). No 2004, dating from 1892, was withdrawn in 1952. Fellow Birkenhead classmates Nos 2008 and 2012 lasted until 1958. Some of the new Hawksworth 1600 class locomotives which were meant to replace the remaining Armstrong and Dean panniers barely outlived them! *J Davenport/Online Transport Archive*

Narrow Gauge

The GWR acquired three narrow gauge passenger and freight carrying railways, all in Wales and all with different track gauges. The earliest was the Corris Railway which was built to transport slate from the quarries around Aberllefenni. Originally a horse-drawn tramway, steam operation began in 1878, by which time an interchange had already been created with the Cambrian Railway at Machynlleth. The GWR acquired the railway from Imperial Tramways in 1930 and abandoned passenger services in the following year. Following some erosion effecting the line BR(W) subsequently discontinued the residual freight services, with the last train running on 20 August 1948. The two surviving steam locomotives which were officially BR Nos 3 and 4 were then left to decay but were snapped up by the neighbouring Talyllyn Railway, along with some rolling stock. They are now Nos 3 and 4 on that railway and for a time No3 was on loan to the heritage Corris Railway (created in 1966) which has restored part of the line for passenger services.

In 1902, the Vale of Rheidol Railway from Aberystwyth to Devil's Bridge opened for mineral and timber traffic and also for passenger services. It was taken over by the Cambrian Railway in 1913, which was itself absorbed into the GWR in 1922. Seeing the tourist potential of the line the GWR immediately built three new locomotives at Swindon, Nos 7, 8 and 9, based on the two original locomotives. Indeed No 9 was originally believed to be a rebuild of the original No 2 but this is now thought to have been a subterfuge for accounting reasons and to meet the GWR directors' requirements for only two new engines. The line has never closed and in 1989 became the first part of BR to be privatised.

BR(W) named the three locomotives in 1956 and, following the end of BR standard gauge steam in August 1968, they became the only steam engines to receive BR corporate blue livery. Back in August 1962 No 7 *Owain Glyndwr* stands at the original Aberystwyth terminus ready to depart for Devil's Bridge. In 1968, the Rheidol trains were re-routed into the disused Carmarthen line's platforms in the main station behind. The carriages, still in use today, date from 1923-38. *Jim Oatway*

Above Wearing standard BR(W) lined Brunswick green passenger livery, the final member of the trio, No 9 *Prince of Wales* dating from 1924, rests at Devil's Bridge in August 1962 before taking a train back to Aberystwyth. *Jim Oatway*

Left The third narrow gauge railway acquired by the GWR was the former Cambrian Railway Welshpool & Llanfair Light Railway. This opened in 1903 to link the rural communities around Llanfair Caereinon with Welshpool, where a W&L/Cambrian Railway interchange was created. The railway closed to passengers in 1931 but freight working continued, the last train running on 5 November 1956. After storage at Oswestry Works the two original locomotives, named *The Earl* and *The Countess* in recognition of a local benefactor, the Earl of Powis, were acquired by the preservation society that had subsequently been formed and which restarted passenger services on 6 April 1963. Following the Grouping, both locomotives were duly "Greatwesternised" which included the fitting of copper-capped chimneys and brass safety valve covers. This photograph was taken at Welshpool on 30 June 1954. *John McCann/Online Transport Archive*

Swindon Works

When the GWR main line between London and Bristol was nearing completion towards the end of 1840, the need for a major maintenance depot was recognised. Brunel and Gooch investigated and found some fields to the north of the railway and slightly to the west of the old town of Swindon. Gooch favoured this location, particularly since it was a junction (with the line to Cheltenham) and construction work started, with the Works opening in 1843. Three years later, locomotives began to be built there. Over the years, the Works grew: the Carriage and Wagon Works on the south side of the mainline were built in 1868 and the famous erecting shop ("A" Shop) was built between 1900 and 1903.

Below On 3 June 1962 No 5961 *Toynbee Hall* and No 5042 *Winchester Castle* were being overhauled in "A" Shop. *Neil Davenport/Online Transport Archive*

Above and below There is still work to be undertaken on these locomotives standing outside on 13 April 1958. No 5219 is a Llanelly-based 2-8-0 tank completed in April 1924 and withdrawn in December 1962. Boiler lagging is under way on Churchward 2-8-0 No 4706 from St Philips Marsh, Bristol and on Laira, Plymouth's No 7905 *Fowey Hall*. *Neil Davenport/Online Transport Archive-both*

Above and below No 4924 *Eydon Hall* is ready to leave Swindon Works for Banbury shed on 13 April 1958 following its overhaul. On the left is one of the GWR's characteristic Shunter's Trucks attached to a Pannier tank with old style cab. Collett large prairie No 6133 displays Swindon's superb lined passenger livery as it awaits return to Slough shed on 13 April 1958. *Neil Davenport/Online Transport Archive-both*

GWR Buildings in BR Days

This chapter may be of particular interest to railway modellers and to keep the pictures a reasonable size for reference purposes, captions have been kept brief.

Above Forty-year old *Pendennis Castle* (No 4079) rests in Old Oak Common's roundhouse in March 1964 prior to its unsuccessful 100mph attempt on 9 May 1964 when the firebars broke at 96mph. *Author*

Right The sub-shed at Marlow, with water tower and hand coaling stage, as seen on 5 March 1961. *Charles Firminger*

Left Langley station, near Slough, displays a distinctive roof style used by the GWR for several single and double storey brick stations. They date from the latter end of the Victorian era, in Langley's case from 1878, and only a few survive today. The Severn Valley Railway has adopted this style for its single storey station at Kidderminster which was modelled on Ross-on-Wye station, since demolished. *Nigel Cox/geograph.org.uk/ Wiki Commons*

Below A September 1970 view of Didcot depot's combined water tank and coaling stage, with the since-demolished Provender Building (food store for all the GWR's horses) in the left background. Driver Brian Wright waves from the footplate of shed shunter *Bonnie Prince Charlie*. *Author*

Right The GWR's coat of arms representing London and Bristol still stands proudly on the frontage of Windsor & Eton Central station which faces Windsor Castle and was rebuilt in its present form for Queen Victoria's Diamond Jubilee in 1897. The station now houses a small shopping centre but one of the four original platforms remains in railway use, albeit truncated. *WyrdLight.com/Wiki Commons*

Below A typical GWR design was the pagoda platform hut. This one at Appleford is being passed by the GWS Vintage Train hauled by No 5900 *Hinderton Hall* and 6998 *Burton Agnes Hall* on 15 May 1976. *Author*

Above A wonderful GWR period setting has been created at Birmingham Moor Street following the restoration of the station building dating from 1914 which was re-opened in 2002. The building was fortunate to have remained intact after its closure in 1987. *Stephen McKay/geograph.org.uk – 1906049.jpg*

Left Codsall station in Staffordshire, some four miles from Wolverhampton, was built in 1849 by the Shrewsbury and Birmingham Railway which became part of the GWR in 1854. The station is still open but the building seen here is now a Public House. *Hilary Wright/ geograph.org.uk/Wiki Commons*

Above The goods shed at the Abingdon terminus of the branch from Radley still had a GWR wall-mounted sign attached to it (above the open gate) when photographed in February 1970. *Author*

Below Another example of GWR signage surviving well past Nationalisation was at Culmstock on the former Culm Valley Light Railway between Tiverton Junction and Hemyock, pictured here on 18 June 1960. *Charles Firminger*

Above The delightful terminus at Ashburton, Devon, in June 1967, complete with cattle pens, on the branch from Totnes, much of which has been re-opened by the heritage South Devon Railway, although not Ashburton itself (but maybe one day). *Author*

Below left The running-in board at Totnes station. *Les Folkard/Online Transport Archive*

Below right A one-time base of the GWS and now part of the heritage Bodmin & Wenford Railway, this is Bodmin (General) station and signal box on 17 April 1971 with my 1929 Austin Swallow parked on the platform after the previous day's long drive from West London. *Author*

Above Falmouth station, Cornwall, terminus of the branch from Truro, as seen on 5 October 1958 when it still possessed a station building (since demolished) although the trainshed roof had already been removed. Closed in 1970 and re-opened five years later, it is now called Falmouth Docks. *Charles Firminger*

Below Moving into South Wales, this is Aberbeeg engine shed built in 1919. It was photographed on 12 April 1964, the year of its closure. The depot had no turntable as its entire steam allocation consisted of tank engines. *Charles Firminger*

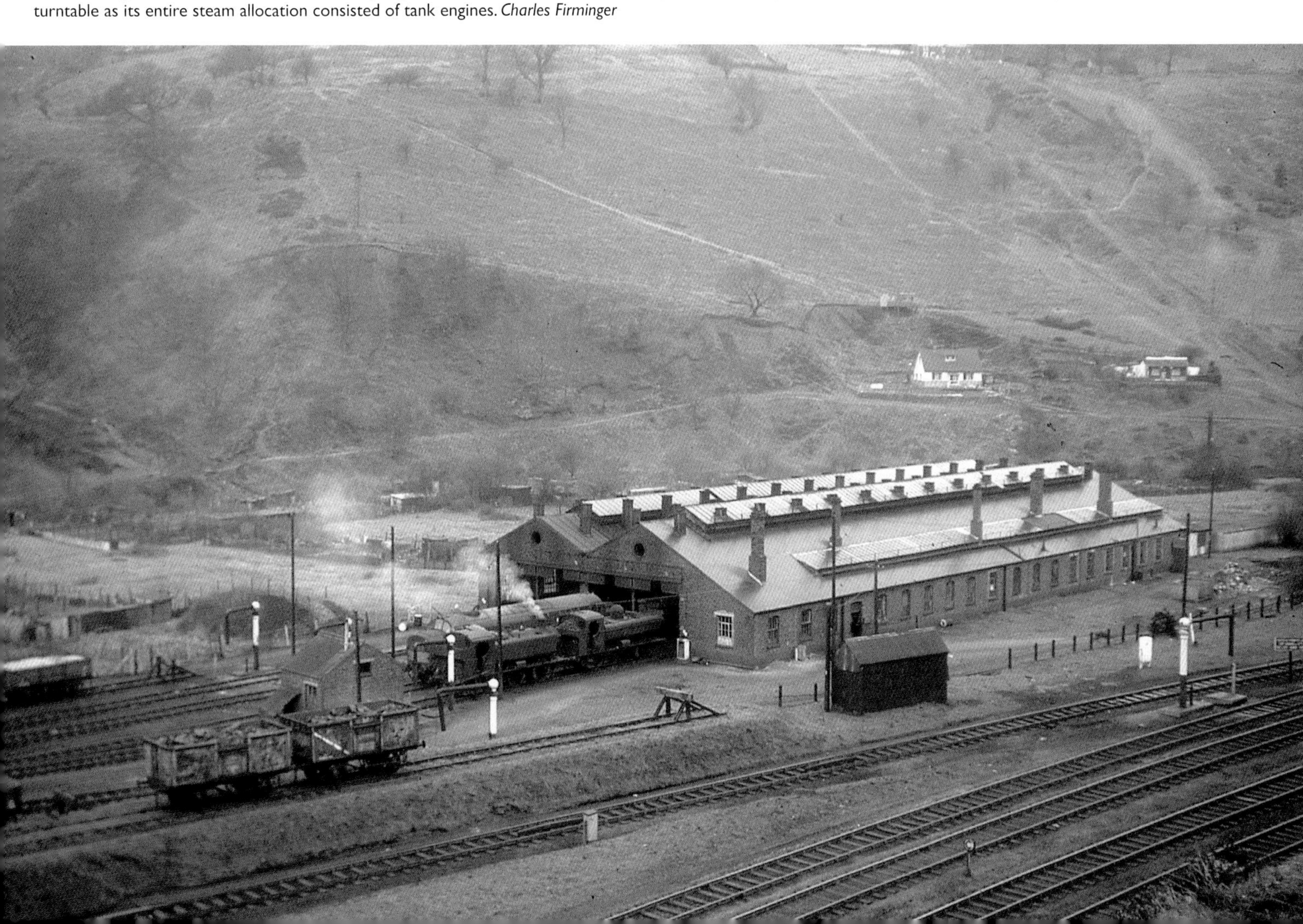

Above This is Chepstow station on the Gloucester-Newport line. Completed in 1850 for the South Wales Railway, the building was designed by Brunel in an Italianate style. *Geof Sheppard/Wiki Commons*

Below This is Bewdley, Worcestershire, on 19 September 1965, once a busy junction with lines fanning out in four directions. Closed by BR in 1970, it was re-opened by the heritage Severn Valley Railway just four years later. *Author*

Above Henley-in-Arden, located on the Birmingham-Stratford line (still open) is seen here looking north on 11 September 1966. The left-hand canopy has since been removed and the running-in board repaired. *Author*

Below Here is a GWR station with no railway, Dartmouth, in August 1959. *LRTA/Online Transport Archive*

GWR Locomotives in BR Service

Above Approaching West Ealing station on 16 March 1962 with the 8.50am Cheltenham-Paddington service is No 5000 *Launceston Castle* which so impressed the LMS when they borrowed it in 1926 for trials that they wanted the GWR to build some for them or to give them copies of the drawings. The GWR refused so the LMS responded by headhunting William Stanier, GWR Works Manager at Swindon! No 5000 also claimed a world speed record for the Cheltenham Flyer in 1931 (see page 98). *Great Western Trust*

Below Glory days for Churchward's 4700 class 2-8-0s occurred in summer 1958 when examples could be seen on the 1.30 pm Paddington-Penzance, *The Royal Duchy*. On 16 August 1958, No 4704 is receiving a final check at Paddington. *Geoffrey Morant/Online Transport Archive*

Above Introduced in 1952 this version of *The Cornishman* was the rather slow 9.15am from Wolverhampton, scheduled to reach Penzance at 5.55pm. Hauled by No 7026 *Tenby Castle* eager passengers prepare to board at Bristol (Temple Meads) on 7 May 1962. *Ian Dunnett/Online Transport Archive*

Below Churchward mogul No 5306 and a Hawksworth carriage arrive at Haverfordwest on 2 June 1962 with the 9.55am service from Milford Haven to Clarbeston Road. Despite this being a sunny June day the footplate crew of Churchward mogul No 5306 have pulled down the cab tarpaulin to protect them from the elements while the locomotive travels tender first. *Great Western Trust*

Above Light prairie tank No 5572, now preserved at Didcot, brings a Launceston-Plymouth train across Bickleigh viaduct. The branch officially closed on 31 December 1962. *Les Folkard/Online Transport Archive*

Below Churchward mogul No 6395 stands at Harlech station heading a train from Barmouth to Pwllheli on the Cambrian coast. The station is overlooked by the castle, much of which dates from its original completion in 1289. *Jim Oatway*

Above With the last 44XX small prairie tanks being withdrawn in September 1955 the larger wheeled 45XX tanks had to be used on the Yelverton-Princetown branch across Dartmoor until closure on 5 March 1956. This view from autumn 1955 depicts No 4568 in the Princetown platform at Yelverton on the Plymouth-Tavistock-Launceston line. *Alan Sainty collection*

Below Devoid of outside steam pipes, Churchward mogul No 6378 prepares to depart Dovey Junction with a local in August 1962. This locomotive was in stock from July 1921 to June 1964. Another aspect of GWR Style is represented here by the lower quadrant signals. *Jim Oatway*

Above This is the last day of passenger services on the former Wellington–Craven Arms line in Shropshire, 21 July 1962, and Pannier tank No 9639 has just pulled into Horsehay & Dawley, now the working base of the heritage Telford Steam Railway. *Charles Firminger*

Left Allocated to Ebbw Junction (Newport), Collett 2-8-0 No 3800 hauls an up freight past the milk sidings at West Ealing on 9 May 1962. *Great Western Trust*

Above Castle class No 5075 *Wellington* and 0-4-2 tank No 1451 stand at Exeter shed against the backdrop of the brick coaling stage in August 1959.

Right Approved privately-owned locomotives were permitted to run on BR up to August 1968. An example was No 4079 *Pendennis Castle* which was privately purchased and kept for a time at Southall depot where this picture was taken in August 1965. The locomotive is currently being returned to main line running at Didcot. *Author*

The lined-black livery of non-express passenger classes before the WR's change to lined "green" is represented in this view of No 4978 *Westwood Hall*. The location is Plymouth (Laira) shed, seen on 25 April 1956. Hawksworth pannier No 8426 and No 7820 *Dinmore Manor* are visible in the background. *Photographer unknown/Martin Jenkins collection/Online Transport Archive*

Despite the official end of Western Region steam considerable goodwill towards preservationists continued at local level (before the steam ban from August 1968 was introduced). This is illustrated in this picture of a train of GWS stock being assembled at Laira (Plymouth) to be hauled to Didcot by Nos 6998 *Burton Agnes Hall* and 0-4-2 tank No 1466 on 2 December 1967. *Les Folkard/Online Transport Archive*

Ex-GWR Industrial Locomotives

Several ex-GWR locomotives survive today in preservation through being sold for industrial use including some rare "absorbed" examples disposed of soon after the Grouping as well as, latterly, more prosaic types such as standard pannier tanks. Here are two examples.

Left Starting work for the GWR in 1930, this old-style pannier tank built by the North British Loco Co, No 7754, was sold by BR to the National Coal Board in 1959 and was withdrawn at Mountain Ash Colliery in 1975. It can now be found on the heritage Llangollen Railway. This view shows it working at Talywain Colliery in South Wales in October 1969. *Roy Hobbs/Online Transport Archive*

Below London Transport purchased thirteen old style (ie smaller-cabbed) pannier tanks between 1956 and 1963, choosing this type rather than later ones because they were a better fit for tunnels. This is No 7760, another North British product, in its guise of L90 after arriving at Croxley Tip with a waste train from Neasden on 11 January 1968. One of LT's last three panniers, L90 was withdrawn on 6 June 1971 and now lives at Tyseley Locomotive Works. *Peter Zabek*

The Preservation Scene

BR(W) was the first region to eliminate steam traction entirely, the official date being 31 December 1965. However, No 6998 *Burton Agnes Hall* hauled the last public passenger service on 3 January 1966 when it ran from Oxford to Banbury, after which it was purchased by the GWS for £2,500. A few GWR engines continued to operate on the London Midland Region, the last three (pannier tanks) being withdrawn in November 1966. Occasional special steam workings were still allowed but this came to an abrupt halt with the implementation of a universal steam ban following BR's Farewell to Steam 15 guinea special on 11 August 1968, save for the Vale of Rheidol railway. The only official exceptions were Flying Scotsman, under a previously agreed contract, and No 1466 to fulfil obligations to operate on the Wallingford branch on 21 September 1968. A lacuna of three years then followed until Peter Prior of HP Bulmer Ltd was able to convince the BR Board to allow No 6000 *King George V* to haul a promotional train in October 1971 and secure a relaxation of the ban. This opened the door to mainline steam being allowed on specified routes with approved locomotives in 1972.

No 6000 makes one of its triumphant Return to Steam Bulmer trips in October 1971. *John Herting/Online Transport Archive*

Right Since preservation Collett 0-6-0 No 3205 has spent time on the South Devon Railway (to which it has now returned) as well as the Severn Valley and West Somerset Railways. Built in 1946, it is seen here on the Severn Valley Railway passing two former GWR Departmental vehicles. These were often coupled in pairs forming part of breakdown sets. GW 118 is a riding van and 112 is a tool van, both dating from 1904. They came as a pair from Stourbridge, arriving on the Severn Valley Railway in 1968. *John Herting/Online Transport Archive*

Below This picture captures a rare event: the GWR's only two surviving outside framed locomotives, No 3217 *Earl of Berkeley* and No 3440 *City of Truro*, working together. They are seen at Didcot in June 1989. *Author*

Left The existing Didcot running shed, Lifting Shop and Coaling stage, were built in 1932, replacing an earlier depot. This timeless shot from early 1977 exudes 1930s atmosphere and depicts 5900 *Hinderton Hall* and pannier tank No 3738, with the combined coaling stage and water tower in the background to the right. *Author*

Below On 18 July 2015, the interior of the running shed appears particularly evocative of 1948 as No 4144 in initial BR livery stands with Nos 5572 and 3650. This initial style of lettering was created by BR(W) based on the GWR typeface because a new national livery had yet to be announced. *Frank Dumbleton*

Right Barry scrapyard escapee No 6023 *King Edward II* has been retro-fitted with single blastpipe and chimney and is therefore the only one of the three surviving Kings which can authentically wear GWR or early BR passenger blue livery. In this view at Didcot, the locomotive is hauling Collett Travelling Post Office coach No 814 dating from 1940 which is demonstrating a simultaneous lineside mail delivery and pick up at speed.

Below This idyllic scene at Highley on the Severn Valley Railway depicts Mike Little's Collett auto-trailer No 178 attached to his 0-4-2 tank No 1450 in September 2016. The station was opened in 1862 and closed by BR on 8 September 1963, but luckily survived intact. *Frank Dumbleton-both*

The final picture in this book features an outstanding performer on the main line, Castle class 4-6-0 No 5043 *Earl of Mount Edgcumbe*, built in 1936 and one of Tyseley's trio of Castles. This example was bought from Woodhams scrapyard to provide spares but a change of heart saw it restored rather than cannibalised, a wise decision as No 5043 has earned a reputation for being a very fast and reliable machine. Forming part of Vintage Trains' main line stud of GWR locomotives, it is notable for having hauled at least two special trains so far ahead of schedule that many spectators/photographers missed it coming through! On 17 April 2010, as part of the GWR 175th Anniversary celebrations it hauled the first non-stop train between Paddington-Bristol since the end of steam working of the *Bristolian* and on its return to Paddington it arrived 44 minutes early, despite being limited to an official maximum speed of 75mph. In fact this actual engine was recorded as having achieved 98mph when it hauled the *Bristolian* on 3 June 1958, the scheduled time for the train being 105mins. On the 2010 run, No 5043 took only 5mins longer. The photograph on this page was taken near Didcot on 11 May 2013 on a special to commemorate the World's Fastest Train, the *Cheltenham Flyer*. The original *Flyer* only ran in one direction (from Cheltenham) but this special did a return trip, arriving at Paddington some 40mins early and Gloucester some 50mins early. After a slow departure from Paddington due to volume of traffic, the 32 miles from Acton to Reading (passing through) took just 26½mins. Again, this was most impressive considering the 75mph limit and the fact that it was hauling 385 tons including a water carrier (behind the engine), due to the absence of water troughs. *Frank Dumbleton*